P9-BYC-352

delicious dips

delicious dips

By Diane Morgan

Photographs by Joyce Oudkerk Pool

CHRONICLE BOOKS

SAN FRANCISCO

Text copyright © 2004 by Diane Morgan.

Photographs copyright © 2004 by Joyce Oudkerk Pool

All rights reserved. No part of this book may be reproduced in any form without written permission from the publisher.

Library of Congress Cataloging-in-Publication Data available.

ISBN-10: 0-8118-4220-7
ISBN-13: 978-0-8118-4220-4

Manufactured in China

Design and Typesetting by Efrat Rafaeli

Prop styling by Carol Hacker and Tabletop Prop

Food styling by Pouké

Photography Assistants: Shana Lopes and Anne-Mette Thunem Herre

10 9 8

Chronicle Books LLC
680 Second Street
San Francisco, California 94107
www.chroniclebooks.com

Cherry Garcia ice cream is a registered trademark of Ben and Jerry's Homemade Holdings, Inc.; Lawry's seasoned salt is a registered trademark of Lawry's Foods, Inc.; Pillsbury Chocolate Chunk Thick'n Fudgy Deluxe Brownie mix is a registered trademark of The Pillsbury Co.; Scharffen Berger chocolate is a registered trademark of SVS Chocolate LLC; Skippy Super Chunk peanut butter is a registered trademark of CPC/Best Foods; Valrhona chocolate is a registered trademark of Valrhona S.A.

Dedication

To Greg, Eric, and Molly—always ready for dips and chips.

Acknowledgments

From munchies to crunchies and all the delectable dippers worthy of a dunk, *Delicious Dips* has been another terrific cookbook project. For me, there is nothing more fun than experimenting and playing in the kitchen. For instance, deciding that I wanted to create an Asian-style shrimp dip meant scanning my pantry shelves, surveying the contents of my refrigerator, and shopping at the market to develop and think about interesting pairings and textures. Sometimes, when I'm creating recipes, I have a solid idea, perhaps trying to duplicate a fabulous entrée I ate in a restaurant. Other times, reading a magazine or seeing food artfully photographed might be the inspiration for a dish. What I *can* say is that food is always on my mind. I have friends, workout partners, and aspiring cooks say to me, "I can't believe you get to do this for a living." I do feel blessed and, perhaps, lucky that I've been able to turn a lifelong passion into my vocation. I have many to thank for the opportunities I've had.

My editor and dear friend Bill LeBlond is clearly at the top of my list, for giving me such skilled professional guidance, support, and time. The cycle of developing ideas, testing recipes repeatedly, and then writing always has its joys, dramas, and challenges. It is a delight to have an editor who always smooths the way.

To Amy Treadwell, Holly Burrows, Leslie Jonath, Michele Fuller, Michael Weisberg, Kendra Kallan, and the others at Chronicle Books who have inspired, supported, publicized, and otherwise kept my projects on track—I am delighted, absolutely delighted to be working with you. To Carolyn Krebs, my copy editor, many thanks for your meticulous attention to detail editing this book.

To Cheryl Russell, my valued and beloved assistant, I truly don't know what I would do without you. At times I have teased and called you my "wife," but it is uncanny the number of instances you have anticipated my needs and supported my efforts even before I asked. It is a pleasure to have you in my kitchen and share in my work.

To my friends Peter and Harriet Watson and their children, David and Eric, and Eric's wife, Paola, I treasure our friendship and relish every meal we get to share together. For Margie and Ken Sanders, Steve and Marci Taylor, Mary Barber, Sara Whiteford, Toni Allegra, Tori Ritchie, Summer Jameson, Josie Jimenez, Priscilla and John Longfield, Laurie Turney, Roxanne Murata and Austin Huang, and Adrienne and Robert Silveria, many thanks for all your support and wonderful friendship.

To my husband, Greg, whose palate I trust, insights I welcome, and twenty-five years of love and marriage I cherish.

Finally, to my children, Eric and Molly, I couldn't have done this book without your energy, enthusiasm, and love. You always challenge me, question me, and make me laugh. Eric, as you head off to college, I don't know what I'm going to do without your well-honed skills as a taster. I guess I'll be mailing you my nonperishable recipe successes. Molly, keep asking your friends for dinner and making suggestions. I value your palate and love your company.

Contents

Introduction

I don't know how they do it—at cocktails parties, that is. Women, especially, holding wine glass in one hand, cocktail napkin or plate in the other hand, and niftily plucking hors d'oeuvres off a passed silver tray, all the while clutching an elegant little purse under her arm. Men, of course, *sans* purse, have one less thing to worry about, but it's a juggling act nonetheless. The bigger challenge comes when a cocktail glass replaces the wine glass. One tiny bump from a passerby sends the cosmo or martini sloshing over the side of the glass, splashing the new, or freshly dry-cleaned, cocktail attire of a neighboring guest.

Is it obvious that I'm a bit of a social observer? Of course, I'm fully engaged, even enthralled at times, by cocktail conversation, but I can't help observing the skills needed to simultaneously eat, hold a glass, and conduct sparkling conversation at such affairs. The food alone can pose quite a challenge. Those one-bite-fits-all hors d'oeuvres aren't always one bite. Nor are they conveniently tidy. Too big, and those topped-toast-point savories shatter upon the first bite. Too runny, and those Parmesan cheese–stuffed mushrooms ooze juice between the fingers. Too crispy, and those phyllo-wrapped triangles send cascades of flakes to the floor.

I'm not really a klutz; my husband and friends can attest to that, but I don't manage well at these types of parties. I fear being bumped, dread the thought of a too-crispy canapé, and know I'll be introduced to some charming guest just when I've plunked an hors d'oeuvre in my mouth.

This brings me to dips. I love dips. I wouldn't have written this book if I didn't like dips! Let me tell you why. When I see a dip and a delectable bowl of chips set on a buffet or cocktail table, I can easily sidle up to the table, set down my glass, and have a hand free for scooping and crunching—the juggling act is over. Now, I'm free to chat without the worry of a spill.

Dips allow for social engineering; set out on a buffet or cocktail table, they change the way guests mingle. Put out small plates and individual hors d'oeuvres and guests will walk around a table or move along a buffet, pick and choose to fill their plate, and move away. Set out a dip or two, in different spots, and guests will congregate—happily scooping and crunching as different conversations blossom. Dips become a positive social mechanism—an icebreaker of sorts—for getting guests acquainted. (That is, of course, unless a guest double-dips a half-eaten chip. But who invites those sorts of guests, anyway?)

The same holds true for manipulating your guests when you want them out of the kitchen and into the living room. Set dips and chips on a cocktail table, point the way, and before you know it the group has eased into chairs, settled on the sofa, set glasses on coasters, and begun diving into a bowlful of crispy delights.

Dips are easy on the host—no fussy hors d'oeuvres to assemble and delicately garnish. Rarely are dips last-minute affairs involving split-second timing and finesse. Most dips are stirred, whipped, or whirled, and then scooped into a serving bowl. And chips are a cinch to make, too. The novice cook can feel relaxed; just make the dip and open a bag or two of high-quality crunchy dippers—tortilla, bagel, and even vegetable chips. Dips are so easy, in fact, the cook looking for fun and play in the kitchen will have time to prepare them *and* the perfect crisps and chips to accompany them.

Delicious Dips includes over fifty contemporary recipes capturing global flavors and tastes. Look at the "Ingredient Glossary, Dip Tips, and Deep Frying Techniques for Chips" (page 12), for an insider's guide to such essentials as handling and roasting chiles, toasting nuts and spices, and roasting garlic. I couldn't call myself a champion of chips if I didn't share all I know about deep-frying and baking chips. Then, you'll see how addictively fun and easy it can be to make homemade chips in "Crudités, Chips, Crisps, and Other Dippers" (page 95).

The recipes included in the book have all been family- and friend-tested. The winners remain; the duds were axed. You'll see classics with a twist, such as the Baked Artichoke-Parmesan Dip (page 22) and the Grilled Eggplant and Garlic Dip (page 36) in "Vegetables and Herb Dips" (page 21). Plus check out sultry lip-buzzing "Salsas and Guacamoles" (page 41) or look to "Cheese, Bean, Legume, and Tofu Dips" (page 57). Hearty meat and seafood dips such as Shanghai Shrimp Dip (page 70) or Chorizo Chile Con Queso (page 78) pack a lot of flavor into a single bowl. For a sweet finale, dip into "Dessert Dips" (page 83) and delight your guests with smooth and rich Caramel and Dark Rum Fondue (page 89), or make the wickedly easy and sensationally delicious Chocolate Mocha Mascarpone Dip (page 86).

To make your entertaining and planning easier, I have included a "Dip Do-Ahead" with each recipe. You'll know how far in advance a recipe can be made, how to store it, and how to reheat the dip if that's what's called for. In addition, I've given you chip and dip pairings for each recipe, called "Dippables." These are my favorite combos for the dips and chips. While I have primarily paired the dips with homemade chips from "Crudités, Chips, Crisps, and Other Dippers" (page 95), I have included store-bought chip suggestions as well.

I say, "Chips ahoy," and get that oil hot for some of the crispiest, crunchiest, most mouth-satisfying dippers you've ever tasted. Unstoppable for eating, unbeatable for taste, homemade chips are a cook's playground of fun. Sharpen those knives, get out the mandoline, and fry up some paper-thin slices of sweet potato, yucca, and carrots. Don't forget wontons, oh, and some tortillas and bagel chips, too. Make it a crunch fest for your guests.

Dip freely, crunch happily, munch on!

■ ■ ■ ■ ■ ■ ■ ■ ■ ■ ■ ■ ■ ■ ■ ■

1

Ingredient Glossary, Dip Tips, and Deep-Frying Techniques for Chips

Ingredient Glossary

■■■ **Avocados** are a tropical fruit, either oval or pear-shaped, with a single large pit. Generally, there are two types of avocados in the market. Hass avocados have a pebbly texture and purplish black skin. Fuerte avocados have a smooth and shiny bright green skin. I prefer the Hass variety because the flesh is more buttery and full flavored. Look for avocados that are heavy for their size and unblemished. Ripe avocados yield to gentle pressure but shouldn't be soft. Ripen avocados at room temperature. To speed the process, put them in a paper bag. Once avocados are cut, the flesh starts to discolor. For guacamole, adding citrus juice helps to prevent discoloration, but the longer it sits the more it will turn brownish. Guacamole is at its best when served within a few hours after making it.

■■■ **Chipotle chiles** in adobo sauce are canned chipotle chiles (smoke-dried jalapeños) drenched in adobo sauce (made from ground chiles, herbs, and vinegar). Look for them stocked with other Mexican foods in supermarkets.

■■■ **Chorizo** is a sausage made from highly seasoned, coarsely ground pork. Garlic and powdered red chiles dominate the flavors. Chorizo is sold either as sausages in casing or in bulk. For the recipes in this book, buy bulk chorizo if available; otherwise, remove the casing from the sausages before browning. Look for Mexican chorizo, which is made from fresh pork. Spanish chorizo, though equally delicious, is made from smoked pork, but is not the type I refer to when I specify "chorizo" in the dip recipes.

■■■ **Crème fraîche** is a cultured cream used in French cooking (and in dips!). Similar to sour cream, crème fraîche is tart and tangy, but a bit thinner and definitely richer. You can buy crème fraîche or make your own. Here is an easy recipe: Combine ½ cup heavy cream (preferably not ultra-pasteurized) and ½ cup sour cream in a jar or small bowl. Stir to thoroughly combine. Cover and let stand in a warm place until thick, 8 to 24 hours. Crème fraîche will keep well for about a week in the refrigerator.

■■■ **Lemongrass** is an herb used to flavor Thai and Vietnamese foods. It has a long, thin stalk with greenish gray leaves and a green onion-like base. The white to pale green inner stalks have a strong sour-lemon flavor and aroma. Look for fresh lemongrass in the produce section of Asian markets, natural-food stores, and supermarkets. Store in the refrigerator, tightly wrapped in a plastic bag. To use lemongrass, trim the base and use the inner white part up to where the leaves begin to branch. Lemongrass is very fibrous, so always discard before a dish is served.

■■■ **Mascarpone** is an ivory-colored, buttery-rich cow's milk cream cheese from Italy's Lombardy region. Made either as a double- or triple-cream cheese, mascarpone has a sweet, slightly acidic flavor. A dollop of mascarpone is tasty enough to eat alone, or with fruit, and it serves as a creamy, tasty base for other flavorings in dips.

■■■ **Rendered chicken fat** is the melted and clarified fat from a chicken. If rendered chicken fat is not available at your local market or delicatessen, you can make it easily. Ask your butcher for pieces of chicken fat pulled from the lower back and thighs of whole chickens. Place the pieces of fat in a small, heavy sauté pan over low heat. Cook, stirring and watching for the fat to melt but not brown, about 10 minutes. Strain, cool, and store in the refrigerator for up to 5 days, or in the freezer for up to 6 months.

■■■ **Roasted garlic olive oil** is usually available at supermarkets as well as specialty stores. Markets are giving over more and more shelf space to flavored olive oils, and it's fun to experiment with the different options. Roasted garlic olive oil adds a subtle garlic flavor to dips. Use extra-virgin olive oil if you can't find a garlic-infused oil.

■■■ *Sambal oelek* is an Indonesian hot chile pepper paste made from chiles, salt, vinegar, and, sometimes, garlic and tamarind as well. It is a fiery paste with bright flavors—a little goes a long way. Other Asian chile pastes with garlic can be substituted, but this one is a favorite of mine. Keep refrigerated once opened; it will keep indefinitely.

■■■ **Tahini** is ground sesame-seed paste, typically available in Middle Eastern and natural-food stores, or in the health-food section of supermarkets. Like natural peanut butter that comes in a jar, there is a layer of oil that separates out from the ground paste that needs to be stirred back in before using. Store leftover tahini in the refrigerator; when tightly sealed it seems to keep indefinitely.

■■■ **Taro root** is a starchy, potato-like tuber grown in tropical areas and used predominantly in West African, Caribbean, and Polynesian foods. Taro root has brown skin and gray-white flesh, ranges in length from 5 to 12 inches long, and can be several inches wide. Look for roots that are firm and smooth. Taro root is sold in ethnic markets, some natural-food stores, and some supermarkets. Taro root should be refrigerated and keeps for about a week. Taro has a nutty flavor when cooked and can be peeled and prepared just like a potato.

■■■ **Yucca (cassava) root** is a large, long starchy root with a tough, hairy brown skin and a crisp, white flesh. It is a staple in Central and South American and African cuisines. Though it varies considerably in size, it is typically about 10 inches long and about 2 inches in diameter. It should be stored in the refrigerator for up to a week. Yucca is sold in ethnic markets, some natural-food stores, and some supermarkets. Peeled, sliced into paper-thin rounds, and deep-fried, yucca makes a delicious chip.

Dip Tips

■■■ **Handling and Cutting Fresh Chiles:** The oils from hot chiles permeate the skin of your hands. Absentmindedly touching your nose or eyes after handling the peppers causes a burning sensation and irritation to the skin. To minimize this risk, get yourself some disposable surgical gloves at the pharmacy and keep them on hand in the kitchen.

■■■ Roasting Fresh Chiles and Peppers: There are several ways to easily roast and char the skin of chiles or peppers, using a broiler, grill, or gas burner on your stove-top.

Under the broiler: Set an oven rack about 5 to 6 inches from the heat source and turn on the broiler. Place the whole chiles or peppers on a rimmed baking sheet and broil, turning frequently, until the skin blisters and chars on all sides. Remove and enclose the peppers or chiles in a damp paper towel(s) and seal in a plastic bag for 7 to 10 minutes. Use the paper towel to rub off the skin. Cut the peppers in half, discard the core, seeds, and ribs, and prepare according to recipe directions.

On the grill: Prepare a hot fire in a charcoal grill or turn a gas grill to high. Grill the peppers or chiles, turning frequently, until the skin blisters and chars on all sides. Remove the peppers or chiles from the grill and proceed as directed in the broiler method (preceding).

Using a gas burner: Set a 9-inch round cooling rack (preferably an old one that you don't care that much about), or the grilling grate from a small hibachi directly on the burner grate. Turn the burner to medium or medium-high, place the peppers or chiles on the rack and roast, turning frequently, until the skin blisters and chars on all sides. Remove the peppers or chiles from the grill and proceed as directed in the broiler method preceding.

Use the peppers or chiles immediately, or place in a covered container and refrigerate for up to 3 days. The peppers and chiles will keep longer if covered with a good-quality olive oil and stored in the refrigerator. Roasted peppers and chiles can also be stored in the freezer, though there is some loss of quality in their texture.

A good substitute when you are in a hurry or don't want to bother roasting your own sweet red peppers is to buy them. Roasted red peppers packed in a light vinegar brine are sold in jars at specialty food shops or supermarkets. Once opened, store any leftover peppers in the refrigerator, making sure the peppers are immersed in the brine. They will keep for a couple of weeks.

■■■ Toasting Nuts: Toasting pine nuts, almonds, walnuts, pecans, hazelnuts, and cashews brings out their full, rich flavor. Place the nuts in a single layer on a rimmed baking sheet and bake in a preheated 350°F oven until lightly browned, about 10 minutes. Alternatively, the nuts can be browned in a microwave. Place in a single layer on a microwave-safe plate, and microwave on high power for 2 to 3 minutes, or until lightly browned, stirring once or twice while they are toasting. Watch carefully that they don't burn.

■■■ **Toasting Spices:** Dry-roasting whole spices in a skillet and then grinding them maximizes the spices' flavor and scent. Place a small, heavy skillet, preferably cast iron, over high heat. Add the spices to the pan and, stirring constantly, toast until fragrant and lightly browned, about 2 minutes. Transfer to a plate to cool. The spices can be ground in a blender or spice grinder, or with a mortar and pestle. Blend or grind until ground to a powder. Lacking any of the aforementioned tools, place the toasted spices in a heavy lock-top plastic bag and pound them with a rolling pin or the bottom of a small heavy saucepan.

■■■ **Roasting Garlic:** Roasted garlic is a wonderful condiment to have on hand. I mash it with a little olive oil and spread it on bruschetta, and add it to salad dressings, tomato sauces, and potato gratins. And, as you'll see, adding it to dips brings a distinctive mellow garlic flavor without the "bite" of fresh garlic. Here's an easy recipe: Preheat the oven to 375°F. Peel the loose, papery outer layers of skin off 2 heads of garlic and trim any roots from the bottom. Cut off enough of the top of the garlic heads to expose the garlic cloves. Put the cut garlic heads in a small baking dish, cut-sides up. Drizzle with a tablespoon of olive oil and sprinkle with a little salt and pepper. Cover the dish tightly with aluminum foil and roast until the garlic feels soft when pierced with a knife, about 45 minutes. Uncover and bake until the garlic cloves begin to pop from their skins and brown, about 15 minutes longer. Remove from the oven and let cool. Squeeze the roasted garlic from the skins. Store, tightly covered, in the refrigerator, for up to 1 week.

■■■ **Zesting Citrus:** Using a hand-held gadget called a zester, the zest (the colored part of the rind, without the white pith underneath) can be removed from a lemon, lime, orange, or grapefruit by drawing the zester across the skin of the fruit. My favorite tool for removing zest is a Microplane, available at kitchen shops everywhere. I prefer the texture of the zest using a Microplane, and with a "tap-tap-tap" of the zester against a cutting board, the zest falls right off the tool ready to scoop up and measure. Buy a zester with a handle, for easier use. Be sure to wash and dry any citrus before zesting to remove any sprays remaining on the fruit.

Deep-Frying Techniques for Chips

Deep-fried chips are sinfully crisp, delicate, and wickedly addictive. What can I say? One bite leads to two, two to three, and before you know it a whole basketful is gone. Your guests will feel the same way—especially if your chips are homemade. It's not that I'm putting down store-bought chips; I have plenty of favorites among them. But for some fun cooking and playing in the kitchen, slicing and frying paper-thin rounds of vegetables, potatoes, wontons, and tortillas until golden, crispy, and crunchy brings sheer satisfaction. There are a few pointers and tips to know, and a couple of safety precautions, but otherwise it is as easy as could be.

■■■ **Equipment for deep-frying:** The vessel you fry in is critical to your success and ease of frying. Choose a deep, heavy pot at least 8 inches in diameter. A wok also works well for deep-frying. However, my favorite way to deep-fry is to use an electric deep-fryer. It wasn't until I started writing this book that I bought an electric fryer, and now I will never go back to stove-top frying. This is not to discourage you, because electric fryers are a bit of an investment (though not too bad as kitchen equipment goes) and there is the issue of storage, but they make every aspect of deep-frying a breeze. From set-up to cleanup, electric fryers eliminate the mess and fumes of frying. They offer the safety of temperature-controlled oil, a splatter-free counter (because electric deep fryers have covers), and a filter that eliminates much of the odor. Finally, the cleanup is easy because a built-in tube allows you to drain the oil easily.

■■■ **Other useful tools for deep-frying:** Use a wire-mesh skimmer for removing deep-fried foods from hot oil. Buy either a skimmer with a long stainless-steel handle and a stainless mesh screen, or look in an Asian market for a wire mesh skimmer with a wooden handle. You'll also need a deep-frying thermometer for stove-top use. Have ready a couple of baking sheets and lots of paper towels for draining the fried chips.

■■■ Tips for deep-frying: Fry in small batches to keep the oil at a constant temperature. Use a generous amount of oil for frying—the oil should come at least 3 inches up the sides of the pan. Always allow the oil to come back to the proper frying temperature before adding another batch of food. Drain fried foods on a thick layer of paper towels as soon as they come out of the fryer. When finished frying, cool the oil and then strain through a double-thickness of cheesecloth. Store the used oil in the refrigerator for up to 2 months. The oil can be re-used for frying depending on how much and what you have fried (beets and carrots discolor the oil). If the oil turns cloudy or dark brown, discard it.

■■■ Safety precautions: Use a deep pot for deep-frying so the oil has room to bubble up without boiling over when the food is added to the pan. Don't over-crowd the oil, for the same reason. Don't drop the foods to be fried from any height, but instead slide them into the oil at the edge of the pan. Use an exhaust fan to remove fumes.

2

Vegetable and Herb Dips

In the culinary universe of appetizers, vegetable and herb dips are the shining stars—they offer millions of possibilities, undiscovered pairings, and galaxies of flavor, both bright and subtle. From onions to mushrooms, and tomatoes to eggplants, these dips will give you the chance to explore an array of exotic and luscious tastes. For summer's starry nights serve bruschetta with deeply delicious Roasted Red Pepper, Sun-Dried Tomato, and Basil Spread (page 23). Warm your guests with the Roasted Butternut Squash Dip with Crème Fraîche (page 27) on chilly evenings when the full moon shines bright. Wander through the recipes, plumb the depths of taste, and let your friend encounter piquancy and spices.

Baked Artichoke-Parmesan Dip

Makes about **4 cups**

Bubbly-hot, runny, rich, oozing with artichoke flavor, and crusty-brown on top—I've never seen a party dip get devoured so quickly. This may be a classic (with a few new twists), but a dip this good deserves to stay in the limelight.

1 large shallot, halved

2 cans (13.75 ounces each) artichoke hearts packed in water, well drained

½ cup mayonnaise

½ cup sour cream

3 tablespoons fresh lemon juice

1 cup grated Parmesan cheese

½ teaspoon kosher salt

Freshly ground black pepper

⅓ cup unseasoned dry bread crumbs

1½ teaspoons finely minced fresh oregano

2 teaspoons pure olive oil

Dippables: Parmesan Breadsticks; Crostini; Pita Chips; Parmesan-Crusted Pita Chips; Bagel Chips; Vegetable Chips

In the workbowl of a food processor fitted with the metal blade, pulse the shallot and artichoke hearts until coarsely chopped.

In a medium bowl, combine the mayonnaise, sour cream, lemon juice, Parmesan cheese, and salt. Add the chopped shallots and artichokes and mix until well combined. Season to taste with pepper. Transfer to a buttered 1½-quart shallow baking dish. In a small bowl, combine the bread crumbs, oregano, and olive oil.

Position a rack in the upper two-thirds of the oven and preheat the oven to 400°F. Just before baking, sprinkle the bread-crumb mixture on top of the artichoke dip. Bake the dip until the bread crumbs are toasty brown and the dip is bubbling at the edges, 20 to 25 minutes. Serve hot.

DIP DO-AHEAD

The dip, without the bread-crumb topping, can be prepared, covered, and refrigerated up to 2 days in advance. Remove the dip from the refrigerator 40 minutes before baking. The topping can be prepared up to 8 hours ahead and sprinkled on just before baking.

Roasted Red Pepper, Sun-Dried Tomato, and Basil Spread

Makes about **1 cup**

Scarlet red, speckled with green, and full of big Mediterranean flavors, this spread is perfect party fare whether you're entertaining on the deck or throwing a Christmas party. Thanks to specialty growers and quick distribution, fresh herbs, especially basil, are in the supermarket year-round—no need to wait for the herb garden to grow. If you are in a hurry or, frankly, don't want to be bothered roasting your own peppers, then use store-bought roasted peppers that come in a jar. Blot them dry with paper towels, dice, and they're ready to use.

2 large red bell peppers, roasted and finely diced (about 1 cup) (see page 16)

12 oil-packed sun-dried tomatoes, drained (reserving the oil) and very finely diced

12 large fresh basil leaves, minced

4 canned anchovy fillets, rinsed, blotted dry, and minced

2 tablespoons capers, rinsed and blotted dry

2 teaspoons finely minced garlic

2 teaspoons fresh lemon juice

4 teaspoons sun-dried tomato oil (reserved from the jar)

¼ teaspoon kosher salt

½ teaspoon freshly ground black pepper

Dippables: Bruschetta; Crostini; Pita Chips; Bagel Chips; Vegetable Chips (preferably zucchini chips)

In a medium bowl, combine the roasted peppers, tomatoes, basil, anchovies, capers, and garlic. Stir in the lemon juice and sun-dried tomato oil, and then add the salt and pepper. Taste and adjust the seasonings. Transfer to a serving bowl, cover, and keep at room temperature until ready to serve, up to 3 hours.

DIP DO-AHEAD

This dip can be prepared up to 3 days in advance. Cover and refrigerate. Remove from the refrigerator 45 minutes before serving. Serve at room temperature.

Cucumber and Radish Raita

Makes **3 cups**

Cooling, minty-fresh classic *raita* gets a colorful makeover with the addition of blush-red diced radishes, undertones of fresh garlic, and the zesty punch of lemon. This is the appetizer of choice for an Indian-themed skewer party. Picture this dip and a basket piled high with seasonal crudités as the accompaniment to a platter of rosemary-scented lamb kebobs, tandoori-style chicken, and a curry-infused rice—casual entertaining at its best.

1 English cucumber, peeled, halved lengthwise, seeded, and cut into ¼-inch dice

8 radishes, trimmed and cut into ¼-inch dice

4 cloves garlic, finely minced

2 tablespoons finely chopped fresh mint

2 tablespoons chopped fresh dill

2 teaspoons grated lemon zest

2 cups plain whole-milk yogurt

2 tablespoons fresh lemon juice

1 teaspoon freshly ground black pepper

¼ teaspoon freshly grated nutmeg

Dippables: Crudités; Pita Chips; Bagel Chips; Vegetable Chips

In a medium bowl, toss together the cucumber, radishes, garlic, mint, dill, and lemon zest. Stir in the yogurt, lemon juice, pepper, and nutmeg. Mix gently to combine. Transfer to a serving bowl and refrigerate until chilled before serving.

DIP DO-AHEAD

This dip can be prepared up to 1 day in advance. Cover and refrigerate until ready to serve.

Feta Compli

This dip's flavor reminds me of *spanakopita,* that fabulous Greek dish of baked phyllo with spinach and feta cheese. What makes this dip so different from all the classic spinach dip recipes I've tasted is the reduced quantities of mayonnaise and sour cream. There's no need for heavy binders—what I love are the hints of fresh oregano, the zip of lemon, and the salty, tangy flavor of feta to play off the spinach, with just enough mayonnaise and sour cream to make it a dip.

½ **small white onion**

1 clove garlic

2 tablespoons fresh oregano leaves

Grated zest of 1 large lemon

1 package (10 ounces) frozen chopped spinach, thawed and water squeezed out

½ **cup mayonnaise**

½ **cup sour cream**

½ **cup crumbled feta cheese**

1 tablespoon fresh lemon juice

1 teaspoon kosher salt

¼ **teaspoon freshly ground black pepper**

Dippables: Crudités; Crostini; Pita Chips; Bagel Chips; Potato Chips; Baked Tortilla Chips (preferably seeded)

In the workbowl of a food processor fitted with the metal blade, process the onion, garlic, oregano, and lemon zest until finely minced. Add the spinach and pulse several times until finely chopped. Add the mayonnaise, sour cream, feta cheese, lemon juice, salt, and pepper. Process just until the dip is well mixed but not puréed smooth. Taste and adjust the seasonings. Transfer to a serving bowl and serve immediately.

DIP DO-AHEAD

This dip can be prepared up to 1 day in advance. Cover and refrigerate. Remove from the refrigerator 20 minutes before serving.

Roasted Butternut Squash Dip with Crème Fraîche

Makes about **2 cups**

I developed this warm wintertime party dip one day while cooking ahead for Thanksgiving dinner. Intending to make soup, I roasted squash, onion, and garlic drizzled with olive oil. I puréed the roasted vegetables, added some spices and a little crème fraîche, and took a taste. Dunking a crisp pita chip in the mixture, I found it made a great dip.

1 butternut squash (1¾ to 2 pounds), cut in half lengthwise and seeded

1 very small yellow onion, cut in half lengthwise, stem and root end trimmed

2 large cloves garlic, skins left on

2 tablespoons pure olive oil

2 tablespoons crème fraîche

1¼ teaspoons kosher salt

½ teaspoon freshly grated nutmeg

⅛ teaspoon cayenne pepper

Freshly ground white pepper

Dippables: Parmesan Breadsticks; Crostini; Pita Chips

Preheat the oven to 350°F. Brush the flesh of the squash, the onion, and the garlic generously with the olive oil and arrange the squash and onion cut-side down on a rimmed baking sheet. Tuck a garlic clove in each cavity of the squash. Roast until very tender when pierced with a fork, about 50 minutes. Set aside until cool enough to handle, about 20 minutes.

Use a spoon to scrape out the flesh of the squash and put it in the workbowl of a food processor fitted with the metal blade. Discard the skins. Squeeze the garlic pulp from the cloves and add to the workbowl along with the onion. Purée until smooth. Add the crème fraîche, salt, nutmeg, cayenne, and a few grinds of pepper. Process to combine and then taste and adjust the seasonings. Transfer to a serving bowl and serve immediately.

DIP DO-AHEAD

This dip can be prepared up to 3 days in advance. Cover and refrigerate. Rewarm in a microwave or on the stove-top in a double-boiler just before serving.

Wild Mushroom Spread with Onion, Caraway, and Dill

Makes **3 cups**

Make this spread for a party or as a starter to a casual supper in the late spring and early fall, when wild mushrooms are plentiful in the market. For this spread, I can't resist chanterelle mushrooms when I see them fresh at the farmers' market, but other varieties work well also. Sautéed with a little onion, mixed with fresh herbs, and swirled with a touch of cream, this topper is an earthy indulgence. If there is any of the spread left over, add it to risotto or use it as an omelet filling.

¼ **cup pure olive oil**

1 medium yellow onion, chopped

2 teaspoons caraway seeds

1½ **pounds assorted wild and culti-vated mushrooms (such as cremini, shiitake, and chanterelle), wiped or brushed clean, stems trimmed, coarsely chopped**

2 teaspoons kosher salt

Freshly ground black pepper

2 tablespoons chopped fresh flat-leaf parsley

1 tablespoon chopped fresh dill

1 teaspoon minced fresh thyme

½ **cup heavy (whipping) cream**

Dippables: Bruschetta; Crostini; Pita Chips; Lemon Olive Oil and Fresh Thyme Pita Chips; Bagel Chips

In a large skillet over medium-high heat, warm the olive oil and swirl to coat the pan. Add the onion and sauté until just beginning to soften, about 3 minutes. Add the caraway seeds and stir constantly until fragrant, about 1 minute. Add the mushrooms and sauté, stirring frequently, until they just begin to soften, about 2 minutes. Add the salt and a few grinds of pepper and continue to sauté until the mushrooms give off their juices, about 4 minutes longer. Add the parsley, dill, thyme, and ¼ cup of the cream to the pan. Sauté, stirring constantly, until the liquids are almost evaporated, 1 to 2 minutes longer. Remove from the heat and let cool for 10 minutes.

Transfer the mushroom mixture to the workbowl of a food processor fitted with the metal blade. Add the remaining $\frac{1}{4}$ cup cream and pulse 5 or 6 times until the mushroom mixture is finely chopped but not puréed. Transfer to a serving bowl and serve immediately.

DIP DO-AHEAD

This dip can be prepared up to 1 day in advance. Cover and refrigerate. Rewarm in a microwave or in a skillet over low heat just before serving.

Not Your Mother's Onion Dip

Makes about **2 cups**

If your mother was anything like mine, onion dip meant opening a package of onion soup mix and mixing it with sour cream. A bowlful of ridged potato chips was set out and, ta-da, chips and dips were ready to serve. Remove that image from your mind; instead envision a spectacular dip for which onions are cooked until softened, sweet, and deeply caramelized and a touch of mellow balsamic vinegar is added to heighten and round out the flavor. Use the time while the onions are cooking to make some homemade chips—including hot-from-the-fryer potato chips.

3 tablespoons pure olive oil

3 large sweet onions (about 3 pounds), such as Walla Walla, Vidalia, or Maui, cut into $\frac{1}{2}$-inch dice

2 large shallots, finely diced

1$\frac{1}{2}$ tablespoons sugar

$\frac{1}{3}$ cup balsamic vinegar

$\frac{1}{3}$ cup sour cream

3 tablespoons mayonnaise

$\frac{3}{4}$ teaspoon kosher salt

$\frac{1}{2}$ teaspoon freshly ground black pepper

Dippables: Bruschetta; Crostini; Pita Chips; Bagel Chips; Roasted Garlic Bagel Chips; Wonton Crisps; Potato Chips; Yucca Chips

In a 12-inch sauté pan over medium-low heat, warm the oil and swirl to coat the pan. Add the onions and cook, covered, stirring frequently, until the onions soften and turn translucent, about 10 minutes. Uncover the pan and continue sautéing, adjusting the heat to low if the onions begin to brown, until the onions are completely softened and begin to caramelize, about 15 minutes longer. Add the shallots and sauté until softened, about 5 minutes longer. Add the sugar and continue to cook, stirring constantly, until the onions turn a beautiful caramel color, 5 to 7 minutes longer. Add the balsamic vinegar and stir to combine. When the vinegar has evaporated, remove the pan from the heat. Transfer the onion mixture to a bowl and cool about 15 minutes.

Add the sour cream, mayonnaise, salt, and pepper to the onion mixture. Stir until completely combined. Taste and adjust the seasonings. Transfer to a serving bowl and serve slightly warm or at room temperature.

DIP DO-AHEAD

This dip can be prepared up to 3 days in advance. Cover and refrigerate. Remove from the refrigerator 1 hour before serving. Serve at room temperature, or rewarm in a microwave or in a skillet over low heat just before serving.

Dip into India

Makes **2 ½ cups**

Here's another dip whose inspiration came from making soup. For my second cookbook, *Very Entertaining,* published back in 1990, I developed a recipe for curried cauliflower soup that is still one of my all-time favorites. When I was developing the vegetable dips for this book I thought about all the seductive aromas and flavors that come from sautéing onions with curry powder, and knew it would make a great base for a dip. Cauliflower isn't an obvious vegetable to use for a dip, but wait till you taste this with the yogurt, spices, and pretty flecks of parsley. Get ready for the compliments.

1 head cauliflower (about 1 ½ pounds), broken into florets, and florets halved

1 ¾ teaspoons kosher salt

1 tablespoon pure olive oil

1 medium yellow onion, finely diced

1 tablespoon curry powder

1 tablespoon sugar

1 cup plain whole-milk yogurt

¼ cup sour cream

⅓ cup packed, coarsely chopped flat-leaf parsley

Dash freshly ground nutmeg

Dash cayenne pepper

Freshly ground black pepper

Dippables: Crudités; Crostini; Pita Chips; Bagel Chips; Fried Tortilla Chips; Baked Tortilla Chips (preferably seeded); Taro Root or Yucca Chips

Fill a 4-quart saucepan with 2 inches of water and bring to a boil over high heat. Add the cauliflower and ¼ teaspoon of the salt. Partially cover the pan, adjust the heat so the water simmers, and cook the cauliflower until tender when pierced with a fork, about 10 minutes. Drain completely and transfer to a bowl.

In a small sauté pan over medium heat, warm the olive oil and swirl to coat the pan. Add the onion and sauté until soft and translucent, about 5 minutes. Add the curry powder, remaining 1 ½ teaspoons of salt, and the sugar, and stir constantly until the curry is fragrant, 1 to 2 minutes longer. Remove from the heat.

continued →

Use a fork to mash the cauliflower into very small pieces. Add the onion mixture and stir to combine. Using a rubber spatula, stir in the yogurt, sour cream, parsley, nutmeg, cayenne, and a few grinds of pepper. Taste and adjust the seasonings. Transfer to a serving bowl and serve immediately.

DIP DO-AHEAD

This dip can be prepared up to 2 days in advance. Cover and refrigerate. Remove from the refrigerator 45 minutes before serving. Serve the dip at room temperature.

Fig and Kalamata Olive Tapenade

Makes **1½ cups**

In this savory spread, the rich taste and intriguing texture of plumped dried figs contrasts with salt-brined purple-black olives, pine nuts, capers, and a hint of oregano. Blended with a dash of balsamic vinegar and deeply flavored extra-virgin olive oil, this tapenade is the perfect topper for bruschetta at a summer grill party. When grilling isn't the party plan, crostini, bagel chips, and pita chips also partner well with this spread.

1½ cups finely chopped, dried Black Mission figs, stems removed

½ cup water

½ cup kalamata olives, pitted and chopped

⅓ cup pine nuts, toasted (see page 16)

2 tablespoons balsamic vinegar

2 tablespoons extra-virgin olive oil

2 tablespoons small capers, rinsed and blotted dry

1½ tablespoons chopped fresh oregano leaves

½ teaspoon kosher salt

½ teaspoon freshly ground black pepper

Dippables: Bruschetta; Crostini; Bagel Chips; Pita Chips

Place the figs and water in a small saucepan and bring the water to a simmer over medium-low heat. Cook until the figs are softened and the liquid has evaporated, about 7 minutes. Transfer the figs to a medium bowl. Add the olives, pine nuts, vinegar, oil, capers, oregano, salt, and pepper. Mix gently to combine. Transfer to a serving bowl, cover, and set aside at room temperature for 1 hour before serving to allow the flavors to meld.

DIP DO-AHEAD

This dip can be prepared up to 5 days in advance. Cover and refrigerate. Remove from the refrigerator 45 minutes before serving. Serve the dip at room temperature.

Grilled Eggplant and Garlic Dip

Makes about **2 cups**

The smoky quality of grilled eggplant gives this dip its distinctive flavor. For this dip, I use globe eggplants, the big purple-black ones you see most often in the market. Look for eggplants that are firm, with glossy skin that is neither shriveled nor has brown spots.

2 medium eggplants (about 2 pounds total)

2 large cloves garlic

1 jalapeño chile, quartered and seeded

½ cup lightly packed flat-leaf parsley leaves

2 tablespoons tahini (sesame-seed paste; see page 15)

2 tablespoons fresh lemon juice

2 tablespoons plain yogurt

1 teaspoon kosher salt

Freshly ground black pepper

Dippables: Crudités; Bruschetta; Crostini; Pita Chips; Vegetable Chips; lavosh

Prepare a medium-low fire in a charcoal grill or preheat a gas or electric grill on medium-low. Pierce the skin of the eggplants in several places with a fork and grill, covered, directly over the fire. Turn every 10 minutes. Grill the eggplants until they are completely tender when pierced with a fork, about 30 minutes. Remove from the grill and cool about 10 minutes.

In the workbowl of a food processor fitted with the metal blade, process the garlic, jalapeño, and parsley until minced. Halve the eggplants lengthwise and scoop the flesh into the food processor. Discard the skins. Add the tahini, lemon juice, yogurt, salt, and a few grinds of pepper. Process the mixture just until combined. Taste and adjust the seasonings. Transfer to a serving bowl and serve immediately.

DIP DO-AHEAD

This dip can be prepared up to 2 days in advance. Cover and refrigerate. Remove from the refrigerator 45 minutes before serving. Serve the dip at room temperature.

Balsamic Roasted Tomato Spread with Garlic Olive Oil

 Makes about 1½ **cups**

Roasting tomatoes intensifies their flavor and concentrates the juices, making even out-of-season plum tomatoes taste good. I love the look of this spread, burnished red with specks of green, and its bright, robust flavors. Though perfect on bruschetta or crostini, consider grilling spears of eggplant as a base for the spread.

2 pounds plum tomatoes, cored, halved, and seeded

½ teaspoon kosher salt

½ teaspoon sugar

1 tablespoon balsamic vinegar

2 tablespoons roasted garlic olive oil (see page 14)

½ cup minced fresh flat-leaf parsley

Freshly ground black pepper

Dippables: Bruschetta; Crostini; Parmesan-Crusted Pita Chips; grilled eggplant spears; Vegetable Chips (preferably zucchini chips)

Preheat the oven to 350°F. In a large bowl, toss the tomato halves with the salt, sugar, vinegar, and 1 tablespoon of the oil until thoroughly coated. Arrange cut-side up in a 9-by-13-inch baking dish. Scrape any remaining juices from the bowl onto the tomatoes. Cover the dish with aluminum foil and roast the tomatoes in the oven for 30 minutes. Uncover and roast until completely softened, 30 minutes longer. Set aside to cool for 10 minutes.

Place the tomatoes and all the juices from the pan in the workbowl of a food processor fitted with the metal blade. Process until puréed and smooth. Add the remaining tablespoon of oil, the parsley, and a few grinds of pepper. Pulse several times to combine. Taste and adjust the seasonings. Transfer to a serving bowl, cover, and keep at room temperature until ready to serve, up to 2 hours.

DIP DO-AHEAD

This spread can be prepared up to 5 days in advance. Cover and refrigerate. Bring to room temperature before serving.

I Can't Believe It's Peanut Butter

 Makes about **2 ½ cups**

While growing up, celery stuffed with peanut butter was one of my favorite after-school snacks. For a previous cookbook, *The Basic Gourmet Entertains,* I took the peanut-butter-stuffed-celery theme, added a mix of Asian flavors, and developed this recipe for a cocktail party menu. Everyone loved it and couldn't believe the cocktail nibble used Skippy Super Chunk peanut butter. I had to include the recipe in this book, too.

Refrigerating this Asian spread seems to diminish the bright ginger and chile flavors, so make this spread the day of the party. It can be made hours ahead, so there is no last-minute fussing. In addition, it is so quick to make that washing the food processor bowl takes longer than combining the ingredients!

5 slices peeled fresh ginger root (about the size of a quarter)

2 green onions, including green tops, cut into ½-inch lengths

3 large cloves garlic

1 tablespoon sugar

1 teaspoon red pepper flakes

2 cups Skippy Super Chunk peanut butter

¼ cup low-sodium soy sauce

2 tablespoons Asian sesame oil

Dippables: Celery sticks and other crudités; Bagel Chips; Salty Wonton Crisps; Taro Root Chips

In the workbowl of a food processor fitted with the metal blade, process the ginger, green onions, garlic, sugar, and red pepper flakes until minced. Add the peanut butter, soy sauce, and sesame oil. Process until all the ingredients are well combined. Transfer to a serving bowl. Cover and set aside at room temperature until ready to serve.

DIP DO-AHEAD

This dip can be prepared up to 8 hours in advance.

3

Salsas and Guacamoles

Invigorating flavors, fragrant fruits, intoxicating chiles, and dreamy-creamy avocados define this selection of salsas and guacamoles. Think of these as a fiesta of exciting party possibilities—hip-swaying salsa for music-filled nights, cooling complements to a barbecue bash, or jump-starts for a beer-and-chili gathering.

Fire-Roasted Corn and Sweet Red Pepper Salsa

Makes about **3 cups**

Shucks, I just love corn—especially the supersweet varieties—because I can buy it almost year-round and it's crunchy and sweet, not bland and starchy. Of course, fresh corn from the farmers' market is ideal, but the season is short. Grilling the corn until it is slightly charred, with just a tinge of mahogany color, is what gives this salsa its distinctive flavor. Studded with diced red pepper and green onion, this salsa has all the right moves for a peppy party.

3 ears fresh corn, husks on

Vegetable oil for brushing

$\frac{1}{2}$ teaspoon Kosher salt, plus extra for the corn

Freshly ground black pepper

1 red bell pepper, seeded, deribbed, and cut into $\frac{1}{4}$ - inch dice

4 green onions, including green tops, cut into $\frac{1}{4}$ - inch dice

4 canned chipotle chiles in adobo sauce, minced, plus 1 tablespoon of the adobo sauce (see page 13)

2 tablespoons fresh lime juice

1 teaspoon sugar

Dippables: Fried Tortilla Chips, Baked Tortilla Chips; store-bought tortilla chips or corn chips; Pita Chips; Bagel Chips

Prepare a medium-hot fire in a charcoal grill or preheat a gas or electric grill on medium-high.

Pull back the husk from each ear of corn without actually removing it. Remove the silk, and then brush each ear of corn lightly with oil. Sprinkle the corn lightly with salt and pepper. Re-cover the corn with the husk, and then twist the husks at the top to close.

When the grill is hot, arrange the corn on the grill grate directly over the fire. Cover the grill and cook the corn on one side, about 5 minutes. Turn the corn and cover the grill again. Give the corn one more turn and continue grilling just until the corn begins picking up color without blackening, about 2 minutes longer. Remove the corn from the grill.

When the corn is cool enough to handle, remove the husks. Working with 1 ear at a time, stand it upright, stem-end down, on a cutting board. Using a sharp knife, cut downward along the cob, removing the kernels and rotating the cob a quarter-turn after each cut. Discard the cobs and scoop the kernels into a large bowl. Add the bell pepper, green onions, chiles, adobo sauce, lime juice, sugar, and $\frac{1}{2}$ teaspoon salt. Stir gently to combine. Transfer to a serving bowl and serve immediately.

DIP DO-AHEAD

The dip can be prepared up to 2 days in advance. Cover and refrigerate. Remove from the refrigerator 45 minutes before serving. Serve the salsa at room temperature.

Paola's Mango Salsa with Cilantro

Makes about **3 cups**

My friend Paola Gentry gave me this recipe, and the first time I made it, I knew it was the best mango salsa I'd ever had. She learned it from her mother, who is originally from a little town in Colombia called Rionegro, not far from Medellín. Paola advises, "Of course, use it as a salsa with chips, but I can eat it plain, just give me a spoon. And, if mangoes aren't ripe but peaches or nectarines are in season, it's terrific with those fruits, too."

2 mangoes, peeled, pitted, and cut into ½-inch dice

½ medium red onion, cut into ¼-inch dice

4 green onions, including green tops, diced

2 tomatoes, cored, seeded, and cut into ½-inch dice

1 jalapeño chile, seeds and ribs removed, finely minced

1 cup chopped fresh cilantro leaves

Juice of 1 large lemon

Juice of 1 lime

2 tablespoons pure olive oil

1 teaspoon kosher salt

Dippables: Fried Tortilla Chips, Baked Tortilla Chips; store-bought tortilla chips or corn chips; Pita Chips; Salty Wonton Crisps; Taro Root Chips; Yucca Chips

In a medium bowl, combine the mangoes, red onion, green onions, tomatoes, jalapeño, and cilantro. In a measuring cup, stir together the lemon juice, lime juice, oil, and salt. Stir until the salt dissolves, and then pour over the mango mixture. Stir gently to combine. Transfer to a serving bowl, cover, and set aside for 1 hour before serving to allow the flavors to meld.

DIP DO-AHEAD

This dip is best when made within 8 hours of serving, but it can be prepared up to 1 day in advance. Cover and refrigerate. Remove from the refrigerator 45 minutes before serving. Serve the salsa at room temperature.

Classic Fresh Tomato Salsa

Makes about **3 cups**

Of course, you can buy any old tomato salsa at the grocery store, but even the top-notch brands won't be as good as making your own—especially with this recipe! My teenage son, Eric, considers himself a salsa aficionado, so when I asked him to taste-test this recipe, I was expecting criticisms and suggestions. But, no! Eric's response was, "Whoa, Mom, this is really good." Check it out!

4 large plum tomatoes, cored, seeded, and cut into $\frac{1}{2}$-inch dice

1 jalapeño chile, seeds and ribs removed, minced

2 green onions, including green tops, cut crosswise into thin slices

$\frac{3}{4}$ cup diced red onion

$\frac{1}{2}$ cup chopped fresh cilantro leaves

$\frac{1}{2}$ teaspoon minced garlic

$1\frac{1}{2}$ tablespoons fresh lemon juice

$1\frac{1}{2}$ tablespoons fresh lime juice

1 teaspoon sugar

$\frac{1}{2}$ teaspoon ground coriander

$\frac{1}{4}$ teaspoon kosher salt

Dippables: Fried Tortilla Chips, Baked Tortilla Chips; store-bought tortilla chips or corn chips

In a medium bowl, combine the tomatoes, jalapeño, green onions, red onion, cilantro, and garlic. In a measuring cup, stir together the lemon juice, lime juice, sugar, coriander, and salt. Stir until the sugar and salt dissolve, and then pour over the tomato mixture. Stir gently to combine. Transfer to a serving bowl, cover, and set aside before serving for 1 hour to allow the flavors to meld.

DIP DO-AHEAD

This dip is best when made within 6 hours of serving, but it can be prepared up to 1 day in advance. Cover and refrigerate. Bring to room temperature before serving.

Black Bean Salsa with Cilantro and Chiles

Makes about **3 cups**

This salsa will be bold and spicy if you include the seeds and ribs from the fresh chiles. If you want a milder salsa, discard the seeds and ribs. If you want the salsa even hotter, use one serrano and one jalapeño chile. If, for some reason, you have leftovers, cook some rice, toss in some grated Cheddar cheese, and make a black-bean-salsa-and-rice burrito. Yum!

2 cans (15 ounces each) black beans, drained and rinsed

4 green onions, including green tops, finely chopped

2 plum tomatoes, cored, seeded, and cut into ½-inch dice

2 jalapeño chiles, including seeds and ribs, finely minced

1 yellow bell pepper, seeded, deribbed, and cut into ½-inch dice

1 cup chopped fresh cilantro leaves

Juice of 2 limes

2 tablespoons extra-virgin olive oil

1 teaspoon kosher salt

1 teaspoon ground coriander

1 teaspoon ground cumin

Dippables: Fried Tortilla Chips, Baked Tortilla Chips; store-bought tortilla chips or corn chips; Pita Chips

In a large bowl, combine the beans, green onions, tomatoes, chiles, bell pepper, and cilantro. In a small bowl, stir together the lime juice, olive oil, salt, coriander, and cumin until the salt dissolves and the spices are blended. Pour over the bean mixture and stir gently to combine. Transfer to a serving bowl, cover, and set aside for 2 hours before serving to allow the flavors to meld.

DIP DO-AHEAD

This dip can be prepared up to 2 days in advance. Cover and refrigerate. Remove from the refrigerator 45 minutes before serving. Serve the salsa at room temperature.

Pineapple-Habañero Salsa

Makes about **5 cups**

Fill your house with great friends, then heat up the party with this colorfully dressed, deliciously hot salsa. Habañero chiles are the hottest of the hot; one was enough for me in this recipe, but add more if you like. Make sure the pineapple is firm, ripe, and full of flavor. Any leftover salsa would be superb with grilled fish or seafood.

1 pineapple, peeled, quartered lengthwise, cored, and cut into ¼-inch dice

1 red bell pepper, seeded, deribbed, and cut into ¼-inch dice

4 green onions, including green tops, cut into ¼-inch dice

1 habañero chile, seeds and ribs removed, finely minced

¼ cup fresh lime juice

2 tablespoons packed light brown sugar

1 teaspoon chopped fresh thyme

½ teaspoon kosher salt

Dippables: Fried Tortilla Chips, Baked Tortilla Chips; store-bought tortilla chips or corn chips; Pita Chips; Salty Wonton Crisps; Taro Root Chips; Yucca Chips

In a large bowl, combine the pineapple, bell pepper, green onions, habañero, lime juice, sugar, thyme, and salt. Stir gently to combine. Transfer to a serving bowl, cover, and set aside for 1 hour before serving to allow the flavors to meld.

DIP DO-AHEAD

This dip is best when made within 8 hours of serving, but it can be prepared up to 1 day in advance. Cover and refrigerate. Remove from the refrigerator 45 minutes before serving. Serve the salsa at room temperature.

Roasted Sweet Pepper, White Onion, and Basil Salsa

Makes about **1½ cups**

Though I call this a salsa, the tastes and ingredients sway this toward the Mediterranean. It's a perfect opener for a grill party centered around Italian or Provençal flavors. For this recipe you need to roast your own bell peppers—don't substitute store-bought roasted peppers from a jar. The task is as simple as could be (see page 16 for roasting instructions), and the texture of freshly roasted peppers is decidedly better than the ready-made alternative, especially for this salsa, where texture and color are everything.

1 large red bell pepper, roasted and cut into ½-inch dice

1 large yellow bell pepper, roasted and cut into ½-inch dice

⅓ cup diced white onion

4 large fresh basil leaves, coarsely chopped

2 tablespoons extra-virgin olive oil

1 teaspoon balsamic vinegar

¾ teaspoon kosher salt

¼ teaspoon sugar

Pinch red pepper flakes

Freshly ground black pepper

Dippables: Bruschetta; Crostini; corn chips; Pita Chips; Taro Root Chips; Yucca Chips

In a medium bowl, combine the red and yellow bell peppers, onion, basil, oil, vinegar, salt, sugar, red pepper flakes, and pepper to taste. Stir gently to combine. Transfer to a serving bowl, cover, and set aside for 1 hour before serving to allow the flavors to meld.

DIP DO-AHEAD

This dip is best when made within 8 hours of serving, but it can be prepared up to 1 day in advance. Cover and refrigerate. Remove from the refrigerator 45 minutes before serving. Serve the salsa at room temperature.

Guacamole with Fire-Roasted Tomatoes and Chiles, Red Onion, and Orange

Makes about **3 cups**

Once when I was teaching a cooking class in San Antonio, Texas, I asked the bellman at the hotel where I should have lunch. His eyes widened and, grinning with a big smile, he said, "Boudro's on the Riverwalk makes the best tableside guacamole." He was right. I watched the guacamole being made and took notes as the waiter gently stirred all the ingredients into the fork-mashed avocados. He didn't measure—it was a scoop of this and a handful of that—so, I guesstimated quantities in my notes, then played and experimented in the kitchen until I got it right.

2 medium vine-ripened tomatoes, halved crosswise, cored, and seeded

2 to 3 serrano chiles

3 large Hass avocados, halved, pitted, and peeled

Juice of 1½ limes

Juice of 1 small orange

¼ cup diced red onion

¾ cup chopped fresh cilantro leaves

½ teaspoon kosher salt

Dippables: Fried Tortilla Chips, Baked Tortilla Chips; store-bought tortilla chips or corn chips; Crudités

Prepare a medium-hot fire in a charcoal grill or preheat a gas or electric grill on medium-high. Alternatively, preheat a broiler and set an oven rack about 4 inches from the heat source.

When the grill is hot, arrange the tomatoes and chiles on the grill grate directly over the fire. Cover the grill and cook the tomatoes and chiles on one side until lightly charred, about 5 minutes. Turn over the tomatoes and chiles and cover the grill again. Grill until the tomatoes and chiles begin picking up color without blackening, 3 to 4 minutes longer. Remove from the grill.

continued →

If broiling, arrange the tomatoes and chiles on a rimmed baking sheet and broil, turning frequently, until the skin blisters and chars on all sides. Remove from the broiler. Dice the tomatoes and set aside. Remove and discard the charred skin and stem end from the chiles. Dice the chiles, including the seeds. Set aside.

In a medium bowl, using a fork or potato masher, mash the avocados until chunky. Add the reserved tomatoes and chiles, the lime juice, and orange juice, onion, cilantro, and salt. Taste and adjust the seasonings. Transfer the dip to a serving bowl and serve immediately.

DIP DO-AHEAD

This dip is best when made within 8 hours of serving, but it can be prepared up to 1 day in advance. Place a piece of plastic wrap directly on the surface of the guacamole, pressing to eliminate any air pockets (this will help keep the guacamole from turning brown) before refrigerating. Remove from the refrigerator 30 minutes before serving, but keep covered until ready to serve.

Guacamole with Roasted Anaheim Chiles and Lime

 Makes about **3 cups**

If you could buy a guacamole as good as this one, I wouldn't have included this recipe in the book—but you can't. Packed with bold, roasted chile flavor, dotted with red onion and bell pepper, and spiked with puckery lime juice, this version will get your attention. Buy the Hass variety of avocados, with their textured black skin, for its luscious, creamy flesh and rounded, full flavor.

3 large Hass avocados, halved, pitted, and peeled

1 cup diced red onion

¾ cup chopped fresh cilantro leaves

¾ cup diced red bell pepper

3 Anaheim chiles, roasted and diced (see page 16)

6 tablespoons fresh lime juice

1 teaspoon kosher salt

½ teaspoon freshly ground black pepper

Dippables: Fried Tortilla Chips, Baked Tortilla Chips; store-bought tortilla chips or corn chips; Crudités

In a medium bowl, using a fork or potato masher, mash the avocados until chunky. Add the onion, cilantro, bell pepper, chiles, lime juice, salt, and pepper. Taste and adjust the seasoning. Transfer the dip to a serving bowl and place a piece of plastic wrap directly on the surface of the guacamole, pressing to eliminate any air pockets (this will help keep the guacamole from turning brown). Serve at room temperature.

DIP DO-AHEAD

This dip is best when made within 8 hours of serving, but it can be prepared up to 1 day in advance. Cover and refrigerate. Remove from the refrigerator 30 minutes before serving, but keep covered until ready to serve.

4

Cheese, Bean, Legume, and Tofu Dips

With cheese, beans, legumes, and tofu as the building blocks, one-dip wonders emerge as you blend intriguing spices, delicate herbs, garlic infusions, and powerful jolts of fresh chiles. Substantial, nutritious, and high in protein, these dips take you on a flavor excursion through America, India, France, Mexico, and Lebanon.

Goat Cheese, Chive, and Pistachio Spread

Makes about **1 cup**

The better the goat cheese, the better the spread. Look for artisanal and farmstead goat cheeses—almost every farmers' market I've been to has some local purveyors. However, please don't think that commercial goat cheeses won't work—I developed and tested this recipe using several different supermarket brands and all were good. I prefer to buy pistachios in the shell because they are fresher, and it seems to me that shelling your own is ample justification for the cook to munch a few. Take off any loose pistachio skins while you're at it.

1 clove garlic

¼ teaspoon kosher salt

5 ounces goat cheese, at room temperature

3 tablespoons unsalted butter, at room temperature

⅓ cup shelled pistachio nuts, finely chopped

3 tablespoons finely chopped fresh chives

Freshly ground black pepper

Dippables: Crudités; Bruschetta; Crostini; Pita Chips; Bagel Chips

In the workbowl of a food processor fitted with the metal blade, process the garlic and salt until the garlic is finely minced. Add the goat cheese and butter and process until combined and smooth. Scatter the nuts and chives over the top; add a few grinds of pepper and pulse 2 or 3 times until combined. Taste and adjust the seasoning. Transfer to a serving bowl. Serve immediately.

DIP DO-AHEAD

This dip can be prepared up to 2 days in advance. Cover and refrigerate. Remove from the refrigerator 45 minutes before serving. Serve the spread at room temperature.

Blue Cheese Dip with Chives

Makes about **1½ cups**

This dip is so simple, so delicious, and so much better than any blue cheese dip that uses bottled dressing. Buy a tangy and rich blue cheese. Two of my favorites are Point Reyes Blue, from California, and Maytag Blue, from Iowa. Though good with crudités and all sorts of chips, for a to-die-for combo, try this dip with homemade Vegetable Chips (page 114).

1 cup (4 ounces) crumbled blue cheese

¼ cup mayonnaise

¼ cup sour cream

1 tablespoon finely chopped fresh chives

Freshly ground black pepper

Dippables: Crudités; Bruschetta; Crostini; Pita Chips; Bagel Chips; Vegetable Chips

In a medium bowl, thoroughly mix together the blue cheese, mayonnaise, and sour cream. Stir in the chives and add a few grinds of pepper. Taste and adjust the seasoning. Transfer to a serving bowl. Serve immediately.

DIP DO-AHEAD

This dip can be prepared up to 3 days in advance. Cover and refrigerate. Remove from the refrigerator 45 minutes before serving. Serve the dip at room temperature.

Farmhouse Cheddar and Tomato Fondue

Makes **2½ cups**

This fondue, though terrific for a party, could be a starter course to keep guests happily occupied at the kitchen table while the cook is at work. Or gather everyone on floor pillows around a cocktail table to enjoy the fondue. A German Riesling is the wine of choice for this. Since you need only a half-cup of wine for the recipe, use a good-quality wine and serve the rest to your guests. The 2001 vintage was stellar and reasonably priced.

1 tablespoon unsalted butter

6 cloves Roasted Garlic (see page 17), minced

2 tomatoes, peeled, cored, seeded, and cut into ¼-inch dice

1½ tablespoons all-purpose flour

3 cups (12 ounces) shredded white farmhouse Cheddar cheese

½ cup dry white wine

Dippables: Crusty-hard peasant bread cut into 1-inch cubes; Pita Chips; Bagel Chips; Potato or Yucca Chips; Taro Root Chips

In a heavy, 4-quart saucepan over medium-low heat, melt the butter. Add the garlic and tomatoes and sauté, stirring frequently, until the tomatoes just begin to soften, about 2 minutes.

While the tomatoes are cooking, combine the flour and cheese in a bowl and toss to coat the cheese.

Add the wine to the tomato mixture, stir once, and then add the cheese, a handful at a time. Heat and stir until the cheese is completely melted. Transfer to a fondue pot set over an alcohol or sterno flame to keep it warm. Serve immediately.

DIP DO-AHEAD

This fondue can be prepared 1 day in advance. Allow the mixture to cool, transfer it to a covered container, and refrigerate. Reheat in a saucepan over low heat and then transfer to a fondue pot for serving.

Curried Tofu Pâté

Makes **2½ cups**

I regularly buy tofu pâté at the natural-foods store when I shop. I spread it on a toasted bagel for lunch, and my children use it as a dip for chips and baby carrots. My goal when developing this recipe was to make a tofu pâté as good as the commercial brand I buy.

1 pound firm tofu

1½ tablespoons pure olive oil

3 green onions, including green tops, finely diced

1 celery stalk, finely diced

1 tablespoon curry powder

½ teaspoon turmeric

⅛ teaspoon cayenne pepper

½ cup mayonnaise

⅓ cup minced fresh flat-leaf parsley

2 teaspoons honey

1½ teaspoons kosher salt

¼ teaspoon freshly ground black pepper

Dippables: Crudités; Bruschetta; Crostini; Pita Chips; Vegetable Chips; Bagel Chips; Multigrain Bagel Chips

Drain the tofu and blot completely dry with paper towels. Let the tofu sit on several thicknesses of paper towels while you sauté the vegetables.

In a small sauté pan, warm the olive oil and swirl to coat the pan. Add the green onions and celery and sauté just until beginning to soften, about 1 minute. Add the curry, turmeric, and cayenne. Sauté, stirring constantly, until the spices are fragrant, about 1 minute longer. Remove from the heat and set aside.

In a medium bowl, mash the tofu with the back of a fork until it breaks into small curds. Add the curry mixture and stir to blend. Add the mayonnaise, parsley, honey, salt, and pepper. Gently mix until thoroughly combined. Transfer to a serving bowl and serve immediately.

DIP DO-AHEAD

This dip can be prepared up to 3 days in advance. Cover and refrigerate. Remove from the refrigerator 20 minutes before serving.

Herbed Chickpea Dip

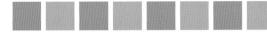

Makes about **2 cups**

This dip is a variation on what you might know as hummus, a traditional Lebanese spread served with pita bread. Minced parsley and an extra hit of garlic brighten the soft, subtle taste of tahini. Smooth and creamy, this dip is best and most easily made using a food processor. Make this dip a couple of hours ahead of serving time so the flavors have time to meld.

¼ cup packed fresh flat-leaf parsley

2 cloves garlic

1 can (15 ounces) chickpeas (gar-banzo beans), drained and rinsed

½ cup tahini (sesame seed paste; see page 15)

¾ teaspoon kosher salt

½ cup fresh lemon juice

Dippables: Crudités; Pita Chips; Bagel Chips; Garlic Bagel Chips

In the workbowl of a food processor fitted with the metal blade, process the parsley and garlic until finely minced. Add the chickpeas, tahini, salt, and lemon juice. Process the mixture until smooth and puréed. Transfer to a serving bowl. Cover and refrigerate for 2 hours before serving to meld the flavors. Remove from the refrigerator 20 minutes before serving.

DIP DO-AHEAD

This dip can be prepared up to 3 days in advance. Cover and refrigerate until ready to serve. Remove from the refrigerator 20 minutes before serving.

Spicy Black Bean Dip with Chorizo

Makes **3 cups**

Big flavor rides high with spicy-hot Mexican sausage. This dip is always a big hit at sports parties. Keep it warm on the stove while everyone's watching the big game, then bring it out for a quick half-time snack with a big bowl of chips and, of course, ice-cold beer.

1 tablespoon pure olive oil

¼ pound bulk pork chorizo (see page 13)

½ medium yellow onion, diced

1 clove garlic, finely minced

1 jalapeño chile, including seeds and ribs, finely minced

¾ teaspoon ground cumin

1 can (14.5 ounces) diced tomatoes in juice

1 can (15 ounces) black beans, drained and rinsed

2 tablespoons minced fresh oregano

Kosher salt (optional)

Freshly ground black pepper (optional)

Dippables: Fried Tortilla Chips, Baked Tortilla Chips; store-bought tortilla chips or corn chips; Pita Chips

In a large sauté pan over medium heat, warm the oil and swirl to coat the pan. Add the chorizo and sauté, stirring constantly and using the side of a spatula to break up the chunks, until cooked through, about 3 minutes. Add the onion, garlic, jalapeño, and cumin. Sauté until the onion is softened, about 2 minutes longer. Add the tomatoes, including the juice from the can, and simmer until most of the juices evaporate, about 3 minutes longer. Add the beans and fresh oregano. Sauté until heated through, 2 minutes longer. Taste for seasoning, and add a little salt and pepper, if desired. Transfer to a warmed serving bowl and serve immediately.

DIP DO-AHEAD

This dip can be prepared up to 1 day in advance. Cool, cover, and refrigerate. Reheat in the microwave or in a skillet over low heat just before serving.

White Bean Dip with Lots of Garlic

Makes about **2 cups**

This dip is for garlic lovers. It is also for cooks who want to entertain but have very little time. With the aid of a food processor, this dip is finished in less than 5 minutes. Add a couple of tablespoons of fresh minced herbs if you like—parsley, oregano, marjoram, or a mixture.

4 large cloves garlic

2 cans (15 ounces each) white beans, such as navy beans, cannellini, or small lima beans, drained and rinsed

5 tablespoons extra-virgin olive oil

2 to 3 tablespoons fresh lemon juice

³/₄ teaspoon kosher salt

Freshly ground black pepper

Dippables: Crudités; Pita Chips; Bagel Chips; grilled eggplant spears

In the workbowl of a food processor fitted with the metal blade, process the garlic until finely minced. Add the beans, olive oil, 2 tablespoons of the lemon juice, the salt, and a few grinds of pepper. Process until puréed and smooth. Taste and add more lemon juice, salt, and pepper, if desired. Transfer to a serving bowl and serve immediately.

DIP DO-AHEAD

This dip can be prepared up to 2 days in advance. Cover and refrigerate. Remove from the refrigerator 20 minutes before serving.

Garlicky Red Lentil Purée

Makes **2 cups**

Quick to cook, tender red lentils take on deep garlic flavor in this dip punched up with a puckery dose of lemon juice, a subtle infusion of cumin, and a blast of chili powder and red pepper sauce. For an all-around garlic fest, serve this dip with garlic bagel chips.

1 cup red lentils

1 $\frac{1}{2}$ cups water

6 large cloves Roasted Garlic (see page 17)

$\frac{1}{4}$ cup roasted garlic olive oil (see page 14)

$\frac{1}{4}$ cup fresh lemon juice

1 $\frac{1}{2}$ teaspoons kosher salt

1 $\frac{1}{2}$ teaspoons ground cumin

1 teaspoon chili powder

$\frac{1}{2}$ teaspoon hot red pepper sauce

Dippables: Crudités; Pita Chips; Cumin and Chili Powder Pita Chips; Bagel Chips; Garlic Bagel Chips

Place the lentils and water in a small saucepan and bring the water to a boil over high heat. Boil for 3 minutes and then remove the pan from the heat. Cover and let stand for 12 minutes. (The lentils will have absorbed almost all the water.)

In the workbowl of a food processor fitted with the metal blade, process the lentils, roasted garlic, olive oil, lemon juice, salt, cumin, chili powder, and hot pepper sauce until puréed and smooth. Taste and add more salt, if desired. Transfer to a serving bowl and serve immediately.

DIP DO-AHEAD

This dip can be prepared up to 3 days in advance. Cover and refrigerate. Remove from the refrigerator 20 minutes before serving.

5

Meat and Seafood Dips

These recipes are packed with layers of flavor, morsels of meat and seafood, and robust, lusty ingredient combinations. Ginger and garlic join forces to transform bits of shrimp into a Chinese delight. Smoked salmon spread lights up the night, wooing your guests with a briny dash of capers, a heady dose of dill, and a splash of citrus. The shamelessly rich liver pâté will please pâté lovers of all ages, especially grandma. These are substantial dips to fortify your guests and keep them content until dinner or through a cocktail party.

Shanghai Shrimp Dip

Makes about **3 cups**

Head to the Orient to relish the splendors of shrimp, beautifully pink and delicately cooked, infused with heady accents of ginger, garlic, and green onion. Their sweet, pungent flavor is enrobed with a hint of mayo and sour cream and a splash of sesame oil, just enough to call this a dip.

1 teaspoon kosher salt

1 pound medium uncooked shrimp in the shell

4 green onions, including green tops, finely minced

1 rounded tablespoon finely minced fresh ginger root

1 teaspoon finely minced garlic

¼ cup mayonnaise

1½ tablespoons sour cream

4 teaspoons fresh lemon juice

1½ teaspoons Asian sesame oil

½ teaspoon freshly ground white pepper

Dippables: Crudités; Crostini; Pita Chips; Bagel Chips; Salty Wonton Crisps; Vegetable Chips; lavosh

Fill a 3-quart saucepan two-thirds full of water, add ½ teaspoon of the salt, and bring to a boil over high heat. Add the shrimp and cook just until they are pink and firm, about 2 minutes. Drain and rinse under cold water. Peel and devein the shrimp. Finely chop the shrimp and transfer to a medium mixing bowl.

Mix the green onions, ginger root, garlic, and remaining ½ teaspoon salt with the shrimp. Add the mayonnaise, sour cream, lemon juice, sesame oil, and pepper. Stir until the ingredients are well combined. Taste and adjust the seasoning. Transfer to a serving bowl. Cover and refrigerate for at least 1 hour to allow the flavors to meld. Serve slightly chilled.

DIP DO-AHEAD

This dip can be prepared up to 2 days in advance. Cover and refrigerate. Remove from the refrigerator 20 minutes before serving.

Italian Tuna Mousse

Makes about **1¼ cups**

Don't even think of calling this tuna salad! Canned tuna never had it so good. Whirled to a delicate smoothness and lightness, softened with butter, infused with a double hit of lemon, and sparked with capers and fresh herbs, this dip is appealingly fresh and vibrant. Italian tuna packed in olive oil is the only way to go. Look for it at specialty-food stores.

1 clove garlic

1 can (6 ounces) Italian tuna packed in olive oil

4 tablespoons (½ stick) unsalted butter, at room temperature

2 tablespoons extra-virgin olive oil

1 tablespoon grated lemon zest

2 tablespoons fresh lemon juice

½ teaspoon freshly ground black pepper

2 tablespoons drained capers, rinsed

2 tablespoons minced fresh flat-leaf parsley

1 tablespoon minced fresh oregano leaves

Dippables: Crudités; Parmesan Breadsticks; Crostini; Pita Chips; Bagel Chips; lavosh

In the workbowl of a food processor fitted with the metal blade, process the garlic until finely minced. Add the tuna, including the oil from the can, the butter, olive oil, lemon zest, lemon juice, and pepper. Process until smooth and creamy.

Transfer to a serving bowl and stir in the capers, parsley, and oregano. Taste and adjust the seasoning. Cover and refrigerate for 1 hour before serving to allow the flavors to meld. Serve chilled.

DIP DO-AHEAD

This dip can be prepared up to 2 days in advance. Cover and refrigerate until ready to serve.

Salmon-Chanted Evening

Makes about **2 cups**

The salmon I use in this recipe is hot-smoked salmon, often labeled "alder-smoked." Delicious and readily available, this salmon has a firmer texture and more pronounced flavor than cured or cold-smoked salmon such as lox. Don't substitute lox; the texture of the pâté would be completely different.

1 pound smoked salmon

6 tablespoons (³⁄₄ stick) unsalted butter, at room temperature

¹⁄₂ cup finely diced celery

3 tablespoons capers, drained and rinsed

2 tablespoons minced fresh dill

3 tablespoons fresh lemon juice

¹⁄₂ teaspoon freshly ground black pepper

¹⁄₄ teaspoon kosher salt

Dippables: Crostini; Pita Chips; Bagel Chips; Rye Bagel Chips; lavosh

Remove the skin and any bones from the salmon fillet. Place the salmon in a large bowl and use a fork to flake the salmon into very fine shreds. Add the butter and, using the fork, work the butter into the salmon until well blended. Add the celery, capers, dill, lemon juice, pepper, and salt. Mix gently to combine. Taste and adjust the seasoning. Transfer to a serving bowl. Serve immediately.

DIP DO-AHEAD

This dip can be prepared up to 2 days in advance. Cover and refrigerate. Remove from the refrigerator 20 minutes before serving.

Just for the Halibut

Makes **2 ½ cups**

Moist halibut is delicately poached in a garlic-, ginger-, and lemongrass-infused broth, then gently flaked and combined with a sauté of oil, onion, and curry, which perfumes your kitchen and paints the halibut with a golden glow. It only takes a few effortless strokes to bind this creation into a spread that delights the palate and pleases the eye. For pure pleasure, bring on the Salty Wonton Crisps (page 104).

8 cups water

1 ½ teaspoons kosher salt

2 cloves garlic, smashed

6 slices peeled fresh ginger root (about the size of a quarter)

1 stalk lemongrass, trimmed to about 8 inches long, halved length-wise and smashed with the side of a knife (see page 14)

1 (1-pound) halibut fillet, about 1 ½ inches thick

2 tablespoons pure olive oil

1 cup diced onion

1 ½ tablespoons curry powder

⅓ cup mayonnaise

¼ cup sour cream

1 cup minced fresh flat-leaf parsley

Dippables: Crostini; Pita Chips; Bagel Chips; Salty Wonton Crisps; Potato Chips; Taro Root Chips

In a wide, deep sauté pan, bring the water, ½ teaspoon of the salt, the garlic, ginger root, and lemongrass to a boil over high heat. Adjust the heat so the water just simmers, and gently slide the halibut into the pan, skin-side down. Poach the halibut on one side for 10 minutes. Using a wide spatula, gently and carefully turn the fish over and poach it until it is just cooked through and opaque in the center, about 5 minutes longer. Remove the halibut from the poaching liquid with the spatula, and set aside to cool.

Meanwhile, in a small sauté pan over medium-low heat, warm the olive oil and swirl to coat the pan. Add ½ cup of the onion and sauté until soft but not brown, about 5 minutes. Add the curry powder and, stirring constantly, continue cooking until the curry is fragrant, about 1 ½ minutes longer. Remove from the heat and cool to room temperature.

Blot any liquid from the fish and remove the skin and any pin bones. In a medium bowl, flake the fish into small shreds using a fork or your fingers. Add the curried onion, the remaining ½ cup of raw onion, the mayonnaise, sour cream, parsley, and remaining teaspoon of salt. Mix gently to combine. Taste and adjust the seasoning. Transfer to a serving bowl and serve immediately.

DIP DO-AHEAD

This dip is best when made within 8 hours of serving, but it can be prepared up to 1 day in advance. Cover and refrigerate. Remove from the refrigerator 20 minutes before serving.

Spicy Crab Dip with Cilantro and Chives

 Makes about **2 cups**

The flavor of fresh crabmeat is so fabulous all on its own that my goal in developing a crab dip was to use a minimum of ingredients. I wanted to highlight the crab flavor and texture, not mask it. Though I keep a jar of *sambal oelek*—an Indonesian hot chile pepper paste—in my refrigerator at all times, I thought it might be too obscure an ingredient to use in this recipe. When I went shopping to see where I could buy *sambal oelek,* my Asian market was out of stock, but my local supermarket had it right on the shelf in the Asian section—yours probably will, too.

1 pound fresh crabmeat, picked over for shells, well drained

2 tablespoons mayonnaise

2 teaspoons minced fresh cilantro

2 teaspoons minced fresh chives

¹⁄₂ teaspoon lemon zest

¹⁄₂ teaspoon *sambal oelek* (see page 14)

Dippables: Crostini; Pita Chips; Bagel Chips; Salty Wonton Crisps; Potato Chips; Taro Root Chips

Place the crabmeat in a medium bowl and flake with your fingers. Using a rubber spatula, gently stir in the mayonnaise, cilantro, chives, lemon zest, and *sambal oelek*. Taste and adjust the seasoning, adding a bit more *sambal oelek* if you want a spicier dip. Transfer to a serving bowl. Cover and refrigerate for at least 1 hour to allow the flavors to meld. Serve slightly chilled.

DIP DO-AHEAD

This dip is best when made within 4 hours of serving, but it can be prepared up to 1 day in advance. Cover and refrigerate. Remove from the refrigerator 20 minutes before serving.

Chorizo Chile Con Queso

Makes **4 cups**

I don't know what the orange goopy stuff is that's served with tortilla chips at ballparks in sectioned, Styrofoam trays, but it sure isn't the real-deal, finger-lickin' *chile con queso* that I know. This is the real deal. This dip is packed with chunks of spicy-hot chorizo, punctuated with fire-roasted chiles, and speckled with bits of fresh tomato.

1 tablespoon pure olive oil

¼ pound bulk pork chorizo (see page 13)

½ medium white onion, cut into ¼-inch dice

2 poblano chiles, roasted and cut into ¼-inch dice (see page 16)

2 canned chipotle chiles in adobo sauce, drained and diced (see page 13)

2 tomatoes, cored, halved, seeded, and cut into ¼-inch dice

2 cups (8 ounces) shredded pepper Jack cheese

2 cups (8 ounces) shredded sharp Cheddar cheese

½ cup heavy (whipping) cream

Dippables: Fried Tortilla Chips, Baked Tortilla Chips; store-bought tortilla chips or corn chips; crusty-hard peasant bread cut into 1-inch cubes; Potato or Yucca Chips; Taro Root Chips; Pita Chips

In a 4-quart saucepan over medium heat, warm the olive oil and swirl to coat the pan. Add the chorizo and sauté, stirring constantly and using the side of a spatula to break up the chunks, until cooked through, about 3 minutes. Add the onion, chiles, and tomatoes and sauté, stirring frequently, until the onions soften, about 3 minutes. Turn the heat to medium-low and add both cheeses, stirring constantly, until the cheeses melt, about 2 minutes. Add the cream and stir until heated through. Transfer to a fondue pot set over an alcohol or sterno flame to keep warm. Serve immediately.

DIP DO-AHEAD

This dip can be prepared 1 day in advance. Allow the mixture to cool, transfer it to a covered container, and refrigerate. Reheat in a saucepan over low heat and then transfer to a fondue pot for serving.

Grandma Rose's Chicken Liver Pâté

Makes about **2 ½ cups**

As if on a mission, I make a point of tasting liver pâté everywhere I travel. Whether I'm eating a refined, fancy liver pâté with touches of Calvados or Madeira, or a deli-style, through-the-meat-grinder coarse liver pâté, I always come back to my grandmother Rose's chopped liver pâté as the best. It's not just my own childhood taste memories that make this pâté seem special; years ago, I catered a reception for five hundred in Chicago and grandma's pâté was the hit of the party!

4 tablespoons rendered chicken fat (see page 14)

1 medium onion, minced

1 pound chicken livers, trimmed and halved

Kosher salt

Freshly ground black pepper

6 saltine crackers, broken into small pieces

¾ teaspoon Lawry's seasoned salt

2 tablespoons Hungarian sweet paprika

¼ teaspoon sugar

2 hard-boiled eggs, quartered

Dippables: Crostini; Pita Chips; Bagel Chips; Rye Bagel Chips; Potato Chips; slices of Granny Smith apples; lavosh

In a sauté pan large enough to brown the livers without crowding, heat 2 tablespoons of the chicken fat over medium heat. Swirl to coat the pan with fat and add the onion. Sauté, stirring frequently, until the onion is soft and translucent, about 4 minutes. Raise the heat to medium-high and add the livers. Sauté the livers, stirring frequently, until brown on all sides but still pink in the center, about 4 minutes. Season lightly with salt and pepper. Remove from the heat and set aside to cool for 5 minutes.

Transfer the livers and onion and any fat and brown bits remaining in the pan to the workbowl of a food processor fitted with the metal blade. Process the liver mixture until puréed, scraping down the sides of the bowl as necessary. Add the remaining 2 tablespoons of chicken fat, the crackers, seasoned salt, paprika, sugar, and eggs. Process until smooth. The texture should be firm and smooth, not stiff or dry. Add a little more chicken fat, if necessary, to correct dryness. Taste and adjust the seasoning. Transfer to a serving bowl. Cover and refrigerate at least 4 hours before serving. Remove from the refrigerator 20 minutes before serving and serve slightly chilled.

DIP DO-AHEAD

This dip can be prepared up to 2 days in advance. Cover and refrigerate. Remove from the refrigerator 20 minutes before serving.

6

Dessert Dips

This book wouldn't be complete without a dip into the sweet side of the party. Sweet tooths, chocoholics, and ice cream junkies will delight as the taste buds explore seductively smooth caramel made deep and dark with rum. Chocolate, luscious chocolate, appears chunked into the Cherry Garcia dip, cooled and blended into deliciously creamy mascarpone, and decadently warm and meltingly rich in Grand Marnier–infused fondue. For those with a tropical palate, delight in a billowy, tangy dip of lime mousse, or feast your eyes on a sunny, colorful medley of fruit.

Cherry Garcia Takes a Dip

Makes **4 cups**

Ridiculously simple, ridiculously fun, and simply delicious, this dip consists of straight-from-the-carton chocolate cherry ice cream, softened and enhanced with more chunks of chocolate and a hint of kirsch, a clear cherry brandy distilled from semisweet cherries. Dip in and dunk.

2 pints Ben & Jerry's Cherry Garcia ice cream

4 ounces bittersweet chocolate, such as Valrhona or Scharffen Berger, cut into small chunks

3 tablespoons kirsch

Dippables: Double-Chocolate Chunk Brownie Chips; Heart-Shaped Apple-Cinnamon Tortilla Chips; Sweet Wonton Crisps; Toasted Pound Cake Crisps; strawberries; chocolate wafer cookies; graham crackers

Remove the ice cream from the freezer and allow to soften for 20 minutes. Scoop the ice cream into a medium bowl and add the chocolate chunks and kirsch. Stir to make it creamy and dip-like. Transfer to a serving bowl and serve immediately.

DIP DO-AHEAD

This dip can be prepared 2 days in advance. Cover and refreeze. Soften 20 minutes before serving.

Chocolate Mocha Mascarpone Dip

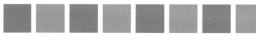

Makes about **2 cups**

Like a mocha cappuccino with a sprinkling of cinnamon on top, this dip is indulgent dessert party fare. It's irresistible with strawberries, delightful with Sweet Wonton Crisps, and wickedness reigns when served with Double-Chocolate Chunk Brownie Chips.

6 ounces bittersweet chocolate, such as Valrhona or Scharffen Berger, cut into small chunks

¼ cup brewed espresso

¼ teaspoon ground cinnamon

⅛ teaspoon kosher salt

1 container (8 ounces) mascarpone cheese, at room temperature (see page 14)

Dippables: strawberries; chunks of banana; wedges of firm, ripe Bosc pears; Heart-Shaped Apple-Cinnamon Tortilla Chips; Cinnamon-Raisin Bagel Chips; Sweet Wonton Crisps; Toasted Pound Cake Crisps; Double-Chocolate Chunk Brownie Chips

Place the chocolate, espresso, cinnamon, and salt in the top of a double boiler and warm over barely simmering water until the chocolate has melted. Alternatively, place the ingredients in a microwave-safe bowl and microwave on high until melted, stirring once or twice, about 2 minutes. Remove from the heat and stir in the mascarpone, a little at a time, until the dip is smooth and creamy. Transfer to a serving bowl and serve immediately.

DIP DO-AHEAD

This dip can be prepared 2 days in advance. Cover and refrigerate. Remove from the refrigerator 20 minutes before serving.

Twistin' in the Tropics Fruit Salsa

 Makes about **4 ½ cups**

Sway those hips for some sizzlin' summer party fun with this fruity, lime-zested, mint-flecked dessert salsa. Cool the palate after a lip-buzzing barbecue with this tropical fruit salsa. Serve with a heaped-high bowl of crunchy, homemade, cinnamon-dusted wonton or tortilla chips (see "Crudités, Chips, Crisps, and Other Dippers," page 95). It's also delectable spooned over vanilla ice cream or coconut sorbet.

1 mango, peeled, pitted, and cut into ½-inch dice

1 papaya, peeled, halved lengthwise, seeded, and cut into ½-inch dice

¼ pineapple, peeled, cored, and cut into ½-inch dice

4 kiwis, peeled and cut into ½-inch dice

2 plums, halved, pitted, and cut into ½-inch dice

Freshly grated zest of 1 large lime

2 tablespoons fresh lime juice

2 tablespoons fresh orange juice

2 tablespoons finely shredded fresh mint leaves

Pinch kosher salt

Dippables: Sweet Wonton Chips; Heart-Shaped Apple-Cinnamon Tortilla Chips; Toasted Pound Cake Crisps

In a medium bowl, combine the mango, papaya, pineapple, kiwis, and plums. Add the lime zest, lime juice, orange juice, mint, and salt. Stir gently to blend. Transfer to a serving bowl and serve immediately.

DIP DO-AHEAD

This salsa is best when made within 8 hours of serving. Cover and refrigerate. Remove from the refrigerator 20 minutes before serving.

Caramel and Dark Rum Fondue

Makes **2 ½ cups**

Divinely rich, and silky smooth, caramel fondue doesn't get much better, unless you add the wickedly decadent duo of dark chocolate and rum. And I did! This fondue is so dippable it is hard to use common sense and know when to stop.

When I call for a large saucepan to make the fondue in, I do mean large and deep. A 6-quart saucepan would be ideal. As soon as you add the cream to the caramelized, bubbling-hot sugar syrup, the mixture boils up, and if the pan is too small, it will boil over. Also, when you add the cream, stand back from the pot, keeping your face away from the steam—it's hot.

1 cup firmly packed light brown sugar

1 cup granulated sugar

½ cup light corn syrup

¼ cup water

1½ cups heavy (whipping) cream

½ cup (1 stick) unsalted butter, at room temperature, cut into table-spoons

2 ounces bittersweet chocolate, cut into small chunks

2 tablespoons dark rum

2 teaspoons pure vanilla extract

⅛ teaspoon kosher salt

Dippables: chunks of banana; spears of pineapple; wedges of firm, ripe Bosc pears; Heart-Shaped Apple-Cinnamon Tortilla Chips; Sweet Wonton Crisps; Toasted Pound Cake Crisps; wedges of angel food cake

In a large, deep, heavy-bottomed saucepan, combine the brown and granulated sugars, corn syrup, and water. Bring to a boil over medium heat, and cook, stirring frequently and brushing down the sides of the saucepan occasionally with a wet pastry brush, until the mixture turns a deep amber color, about 10 minutes. Remove the pan from the heat. Carefully, stepping back a little and with your face a safe distance from the pan, stir in the cream and butter; the mixture will bubble up. Stir vigorously until the cream and butter are incorporated and the mixture is smooth.

continued →

Turn the heat to low and place the pan back on the heat. Add the chocolate, rum, vanilla, and salt. Stir until the fondue is smooth and creamy, about 2 minutes.

Transfer the mixture to a fondue pot set over an alcohol or sterno flame to keep it warm, and serve immediately.

DIP DO-AHEAD

This dip can be prepared 5 days in advance. Allow the mixture to cool, transfer it to a covered container, and refrigerate. Reheat in a saucepan over low heat and then transfer to a fondue pot for serving.

Bittersweet Chocolate and Grand Marnier Fondue

 Makes about **2½ cups**

For those of us whose passion for chocolate is boundless, could there be anything better than deeply rich, bittersweet chocolate melted with cream, tinged with a hint of black pepper, and infused with alluring orange liqueur? (Well, maybe, I *can* think of one thing.) Don't skimp on the quality of chocolate for this. I've mentioned a couple of my favorite brands, and there are others. Go for the good stuff—you'll notice the difference.

8 ounces bittersweet chocolate, such as Valrhona or Scharffen Berger, cut into small chunks

½ cup heavy (whipping) cream

Pinch freshly ground black pepper

¼ cup Grand Marnier liqueur

Dippables: strawberries; chunks of banana; spears of pineapple; wedges of firm, ripe Bosc pears; Heart-Shaped Apple-Cinnamon Tortilla Chips; Sweet Wonton Crisps; Toasted Pound Cake Crisps; wedges of angel food cake

Place the chocolate, cream, and pepper in the top of a double boiler and warm over barely simmering water until melted. Alternatively, place the ingredients in a microwave-safe bowl and microwave on high until melted, stirring once or twice, about 2 minutes. Stir until the fondue is smooth, and then stir in the liqueur.

Transfer to a fondue pot set over an alcohol or sterno flame to keep it warm, and serve immediately.

DIP DO-AHEAD

This fondue can be prepared 5 days in advance. Allow the mixture to cool, transfer it to a covered container, and refrigerate. Reheat in a saucepan over low heat and then transfer to a fondue pot for serving.

Lime Mousse Dip

Makes **2 cups**

Tart, creamy, and dotted with lime zest, this billowy dip made with whipped cream cheese is the perfect partner for spears of fresh fruit, especially strawberries and peaches. For a contrast in texture, don't forget the crispy sweet treats—Heart-Shaped Apple-Cinnamon Tortilla Chips make a memorable pairing.

1 package (8 ounces) cream cheese, at room temperature

½ **cup powdered sugar**

Freshly grated zest of 2 large limes

¼ **teaspoon freshly grated nutmeg**

Pinch kosher salt

5 tablespoons fresh lime juice

½ **cup (4 ounces) crème fraîche**

Dippables: Blueberry Bagel Chips; Sweet Wonton Crisps; Heart-Shaped Apple-Cinnamon Tortilla Chips; Toasted Pound Cake Crisps; strawberries; pineapple spears; wedges of peaches, plums, or nectarines

In the bowl of an electric mixer fitted with the paddle attachment, beat the cream cheese until light and fluffy. Add the powdered sugar, lime zest, nutmeg, and salt to the bowl. Mix on low speed until the sugar is incorporated, and then beat on high speed until fluffy, 1 minute longer. Add the lime juice and mix to blend in, scraping down the sides of the bowl once or twice.

In a separate bowl, whisk the crème fraîche with a balloon whisk until it holds soft peaks. Using a rubber spatula, fold the crème fraîche into the cream cheese mixture. Transfer to a serving bowl. Cover and refrigerate for at least 2 hours before serving to allow the mixture to thicken. Serve chilled.

DIP DO-AHEAD

This dip can be prepared up to 1 day in advance. Cover and refrigerate until ready to serve.

7

Crudités, Chips, Crisps, and Other Dippers

Big dippers, little dippers, and crudités in between, this constellation of crunchy, mouth-delighting bites for dipping and spreading are irresistible. Hot from oven, crisp from fryer, this world of chips will be gone before you know it. Tempt your guests with basketfuls of savories and platters of colorful veggies, and then send them soaring with sweet treats. Galaxies of dips await you and these are the perfect traveling companions.

Crudités

Along with all the crunchy chips that typically get served with dips, a platter or basket filled with prepared, assorted raw vegetables, known as crudités, makes a show stopping centerpiece for an assortment of dips. The best way to assemble crudités for presentation is to think about which vegetables are in season and which will taste best with the dips you are serving, and to artfully pick a variety of vegetables to bring color and texture to the platter.

Instead of listing the vegetables in alphabetical order, I've arranged them in two categories: "Raw and Ready Veggies" don't need to be cooked before they are served, but are just prepped, cut, and arranged; "Blanch, Cool, and Munch Veggies" taste and look better when partially cooked. The blanching brings out their natural sweetness, leaves the veggies crisp but softens their crunch, and gives the green vegetables a beautiful vibrant hue.

VEGGIE DO-AHEAD

Unless otherwise noted, the veggies can be prepared 1 day in advance, wrapped in damp paper towels, and stored in a lock-top plastic bag in the refrigerator.

Raw and Ready Veggies

■■■ **Bell Peppers:** Use red, yellow, or orange bell peppers. (I'm not a big fan of green peppers for crudités. Green bell peppers are underripe red bell peppers and, to my taste, have an acidic aftertaste that doesn't work well with dips.) To prepare the peppers, cut them in half lengthwise, and then remove the core, seeds, and ribs. Cut them lengthwise into long strips about ¾ inch wide.

■■■ **Carrots:** Use whole "baby-cut" carrots sold ready to eat, or buy medium carrots and cut them into 3-inch-long strips. Petite baby carrots, sold with their feathery green tops still on, look terrific on a crudités platter; peel the carrots and leave 1 inch of the green tops on.

■■■ **Celery:** Trim the tops and bottoms of the celery stalks. Leave the tops on the tender inner stalks. Use a vegetable peeler to peel the strings from the back of the larger stalks. Cut the stalks in half lengthwise and then cut the celery stalks crosswise into 3-inch-long strips. As an alternative, the stalks can be cut crosswise on a sharp diagonal into 1-inch-wide slices.

■■■ **Cherry Tomatoes:** Use the larger, classic cherry tomatoes. They are easier to pick up and dip. Leave the stem attached for a pretty presentation. Just before arranging the crudités platter, rinse, drain, and pat the tomatoes dry with paper towels.

■■■ **Cucumbers:** If using seedless English cucumbers, leave the skin on and trim the ends. Cut the cucumbers into quarters lengthwise and then cut them crosswise into 3-inch-long "fingers." As an alternative, cut them crosswise on a sharp diagonal into ¼-inch-thick slices. If using regular cucumbers, peel them, trim the ends, and then cut them in half lengthwise. Remove the seeds using a melon baller or teaspoon. Cut them into 3-inch-long fingers.

■■■ **Fennel Bulb:** Cut off the fronds and stalks, if still attached. Cut the bulb in half lengthwise and use a paring knife to remove the core from each half. Cut the fennel into wide wedges, separating the layers.

■■■ **Green Onions:** Trim the root end, leave the green onions whole, but trim the green tops, leaving the onions about 4 inches long.

■■■ **Jicama:** Cut the jicama into quarters, if whole. Using a paring knife (not a vegetable peeler), peel the jicama by placing the blade just under the skin and pulling the peel away in one whole piece. Cut the jicama into 3-inch-long strips about ½ inch thick.

■■■ **Lettuce:** The leaves from the hearts of romaine lettuce are attractive on a crudités platter, as are wedges of butter lettuce. Even thin wedges of iceberg lettuce give a great crunch, especially to a blue-cheese dip. Prepare and cut the lettuce just before arranging the crudités platter.

■■■ **Radishes:** Buy bunched radishes with their leafy tops rather than prepackaged trimmed radishes sold in a cello-bag. Trim the root ends and leave on about 1 inch of the green tops for an attractive presentation. Wrap the prepared radishes in damp paper towels and store in a lock-top plastic bag in the refrigerator for up to 1 day. One hour before serving, place the radishes in a bowl of ice water to crisp them, and then drain and pat dry with paper towels before serving.

■■■ **Summer Squash:** Zucchini and other summer squash, especially miniature squash, such as baby zucchini and pattypan, taste and look terrific on a crudités platter. For the miniatures, trim the tops and leave them whole. For standard-size squash, trim the ends, cut into 3-inch lengths, and then cut lengthwise into ½-inch wedges. As an alternative, the squash can be cut crosswise on a sharp diagonal into ¼-inch-wide slices.

Blanch, Cool, and Munch Veggies

Blanching vegetables involves nothing more than plunging them into a large pot of boiling salted water, cooking the vegetables briefly, refreshing them in a large bowl of ice water, and then blotting them dry with paper towels. The vegetables lose their raw taste and, in the case of green vegetables, turn a brilliant green, making them most attractive on a crudités platter. The vegetables in this category taste their best when blanched. Approximate cooking times are given for each vegetable. If blanching an assortment of vegetables, you can cook them in batches in the same pot of water, but start with the mildest flavored ones, such as carrots, and then cook more pungent vegetables, such as cauliflower and broccoli, last.

To blanch vegetables: Fill a large pot three-fourths full of water. Bring to a boil over high heat and add 2 tablespoons of kosher salt. Have ready a large bowl of ice water and a pair of tongs, a mesh strainer, or a large slotted spoon to quickly remove the vegetables after blanching. Have several layers of paper towels laid out on a counter for draining the vegetables. Once the vegetables have drained, roll them up in several thicknesses of dry paper towels and store them in a lock-top plastic bag in the refrigerator for up to 1 day.

■■■ **Asparagus:** Use medium-sized asparagus (pencil-thin asparagus flop over and are hard to dip) and trim the woody bases to a uniform length. Peel the stems. Cook the asparagus until bright green and crisp-tender, about 2 minutes.

■■■ **Broccoli:** Cut the broccoli into bite-sized florets. If desired, trim and peel the stems, and then cut the stems crosswise on a sharp diagonal into ¼-inch-thick slices. Cook the broccoli until bright green and crisp-tender, 1½ to 2 minutes.

■■■ **Carrots:** Carrot sticks and petite whole carrots can be blanched, if desired (see facing page for preparation). Cook the carrots until crisp-tender, about 2 minutes.

■■■ **Cauliflower:** Cut the cauliflower into bite-sized florets. Cook the cauliflower until crisp-tender, about 2 minutes.

■■■ **Green Beans:** Trim the stem end only. Cook the beans until bright green and crisp-tender, about 2 minutes.

■■■ **Snow Peas and Sugar Snap Peas:** Trim the stem end and remove the string along the bottom of the peas. Cook the peas until bright green and crisp-tender, about 1 minute.

Pita Chips

Makes **80 chips;**
12 to 16 appetizer servings

Almost irresistible. Pita chips are the one chip not widely available commercially, but they are so easy to make and so crunchy good—whether you make the variations or not—that a batch will be gone before you know it. Guests always seem surprised when I tell them these chips are made from pita bread. Perhaps they don't expect soft pita pockets to turn into crunchy chips. For the most part, pita breads have an easy-to-open pocket, but every once in a while I'll buy a brand that doesn't have a pronounced air pocket. In that instance, cut the pita into wedges first, and then, using a serrated knife, carefully split each wedge in half horizontally.

5 pita breads, white or whole-wheat, or a combination

Position the oven racks in the center and top third of the oven. Preheat the oven to 350°F. Using a knife or your fingers, split each pita bread horizontally in half along the outer edges to form two rounds. Cut each round into 8 wedges. Place the wedges in a single layer on 2 rimmed baking sheets. Don't crowd the pita wedges; it is better to bake them in 2 batches. Bake until lightly browned and crisp, 10 to 12 minutes. Let cool. Serve at room temperature.

Variations

Parmesan-Crusted Pita Chips: Before cutting the split pita breads into eighths, brush each round with olive oil and sprinkle each generously with freshly grated Parmesan cheese, preferably Parmigiano-Reggiano. Cut the pitas into wedges and proceed to bake as directed.

Lemon Olive Oil and Fresh Thyme Pita Chips: Before cutting the split pita breads into eighths, brush each round with lemon-infused olive oil and sprinkle each round lightly with minced fresh thyme. Cut the pitas into wedges and proceed to bake as directed.

Cumin and Chili Powder Pita Chips: In a small bowl, mix together ⅓ cup pure olive oil, 2 teaspoons ground cumin, and 2 teaspoons chili powder. Before cutting the split pita breads into eighths, brush each round with the olive oil mixture. Cut the pitas into wedges and proceed to bake as directed.

DIPPABLES DO-AHEAD

These chips can be prepared up to 5 days in advance and stored in a covered container at room temperature.

Bruschetta

Makes about **12 servings**

Bruschetta comes from the Italian word *bruscare,* meaning "to roast over coals." A specialty of Rome, this traditional garlic bread is made by rubbing slices of good, coarse crusty bread with fresh garlic and then drizzling the bread with extra-virgin olive oil. The bread is then grilled or broiled. Quality ingredients are the key here. Buy crusty, artisanal bread, either a baguette or a large round loaf. I don't use *ciabatta* because the air pockets in the loaf are too big and the topping tends to fall through. Grill the bread so it is crisp on the outside but still soft on the inside. Otherwise, with one bite, the bruschetta shatters, making it quite inelegant to eat.

1 loaf rustic bread

2 to 3 cloves garlic

Extra-virgin olive oil, for brushing

Kosher salt

To grill the bruschetta, preheat a gas grill on medium, or prepare a charcoal fire and wait until the coals reach the white-ash stage and the fire begins to die down to low coals.

To broil the bruschetta, adjust the oven rack so it is about 4 inches from the heat source and preheat the broiler.

Cut the bread on the diagonal into ½-inch-thick slices. If using a round loaf, cut each slice in half, or even in thirds to make appetizer-size portions. Depending on how much garlic flavor you like, rub one or both sides of the bread with the garlic. Brush both sides of the bread generously with olive oil. Sprinkle the bread very lightly with salt.

Grill or broil the bread until nicely browned on both sides but still soft within, being careful not to burn it. Serve the bread hot, warm, or at room temperature.

DIPPABLES DO-AHEAD

The bruschetta is best made shortly before serving, but can be prepared 2 hours ahead and stored uncovered at room temperature.

Crostini

Makes about **12 servings**

Crostini means "little toasts" in Italian. They are very small, thin slices of toasted bread usually brushed with olive oil and baked. To vary the flavor, use herbed or seeded baguettes, and try brushing the bread with flavored olive oils. If you want a plain toast to serve with a dip or spread, then toast the bread slices without brushing them with any oil.

1 baguette, about 1½ inches in diameter

Extra-virgin olive oil, for brushing

Position the oven racks in the center and top third of the oven. Preheat the oven to 350°F. Cut the bread into ¼-inch-thick slices and arrange in a single layer on 2 baking sheets. Brush both sides of the bread lightly with olive oil. Bake until lightly brown on one side, about 7 minutes. Turn the bread slices over and switch the position of the baking sheets. Bake the crostini until lightly brown on the other side, about 5 minutes longer. The toasts should be crunchy but not brittle. Arrange on a serving platter. Serve warm or at room temperature.

DIPPABLES DO-AHEAD

The crostini are best when made the day of serving, but can be prepared up to 2 days in advance and stored in a covered container at room temperature. The toasts will soften if stored in plastic bags.

Salty or Sweet Wonton Crisps

Makes **60 triangle crisps** or **30 fanciful crisps**

Explosively crunchy and a snap to make, wonton crisps are wickedly good. (When buying wontons for deep-frying, look for the thin ones—they result in a better crunch.) They go well with so many of the dips, but a couple of my favorite pairings are serving them with Shanghai Shrimp Dip (page 70) or Spicy Crab Dip with Cilantro and Chives (page 77).

30 (3 - by - 3½-inch) thin square wonton wrappers

About 1½ quarts canola or vegetable oil, for deep-frying

Kosher salt, for salty wonton crisps

Sugar, for sweet wonton crisps

Using a sharp knife, cut the wonton squares diagonally in half to form 2 triangles. Alternatively, use a cookie cutter, such as a star- or flower-shaped one, to cut the wontons. Have ready 2 baking sheets lined with paper towels.

Pour enough oil into a deep, heavy pot or electric deep-fryer, to come about 3 inches up the sides. (If using an electric deep-fryer, follow the manufacturer's instructions for heating oil.) Heat the oil until the temperature registers 375°F on a deep-frying thermometer.

Frying in small batches, add a handful of wontons and deep-fry, stirring once or twice, until the wontons are golden brown, about 1½ minutes. Using a slotted spoon or wire-mesh skimmer, transfer the wontons to the prepared baking sheets to drain. Sprinkle lightly with salt or sugar depending on whether you are making salty or sweet wonton crisps. Continue frying in batches, checking to make sure the oil is at 375°F before adding a new batch. Transfer to a basket or serving bowl and serve warm or at room temperature.

DIPPABLES DO-AHEAD

The wonton crisps are best served within 8 hours of making them, but can be prepared 1 day in advance and stored in a covered container at room temperature. The chips will soften if stored in plastic bags.

Bagel Chips

Makes about **64 bagel chips**;
10 to 14 appetizer servings

There is no comparison between store-bought and homemade bagel chips. Homemade bagel chips are so good—addictively so—that I avoid making them unless company is coming, because I'll eat the whole batch. Plus, they are so simple to make. I love all the possible variations: use rye bagels; herb bagels; sesame, garlic, onion, or multigrain bagels. Rye or pumpernickel bagel chips are fabulous with Grandma Rose's Chicken Liver Pâté (page 80), and multigrain bagel chips are a great foil for the Curried Tofu Pâté (page 62).

Think about making some dessert bagel chips! Blueberry bagel chips are terrific with the Lime Mousse Dip (page 92) and cinnamon-raisin bagel chips are a terrific dipper for any of the dessert dips with chocolate in them, but especially for the Chocolate Mocha Mascarpone Dip (page 86). Be sure to use butter instead of olive oil for brushing dessert bagel chips.

4 bagels

Extra-virgin olive oil, for brushing savory bagels

Unsalted, melted butter, for brushing sweet bagels

Position the oven racks in the center and top third of the oven. Preheat the oven to 325°F. Line 2 baking sheets with parchment paper.

With a sharp bread knife, cut the bagels in half crosswise to form 2 short horseshoes. Stand the bagel halves on their cut sides and carefully slice them as thinly as possible, getting about 8 slices out of each half. Arrange the slices in a single layer on the baking sheets. Brush both sides of the bagels lightly with olive oil or butter. Bake until lightly brown on one side, 5 to 7 minutes. Turn the bread slices over and switch the position of the baking sheets. Bake until lightly brown on the other side, about 2 minutes longer, or until crunchy. Arrange on a serving platter or in a basket and serve warm or at room temperature.

continued →

Variations

Roasted Garlic Bagel Chips: Use garlic bagels and brush the bagel slices with roasted garlic–flavored olive oil. Bake as directed.

Parmesan-Crusted Bagel Chips: Use plain or herb-flavored bagels and brush the slices with extra-virgin olive oil. Sprinkle the slices with freshly grated Parmesan cheese, preferably Parmigiano-Reggiano. Bake as directed.

DIPPABLES DO-AHEAD

The bagel chips are best served within 8 hours of making them, but can be prepared 2 days in advance and stored in a covered container at room temperature. The chips will soften if stored in plastic bags.

Parmesan Breadsticks

Makes **24 breadsticks**;
8 to 12 appetizer servings

Crisp, crunchy, and warm from the oven, nothing beats these easy-to-make Parmesan-crusted breadsticks. You can use thawed frozen pizza dough instead of the puff pastry, and make a softer cheese-crusted breadstick, but I love the flaky, brittle bite of these. Double the recipe for a crowd—these are gone before you know it!

1 package (17.3 ounces) frozen puff pastry sheets

4 tablespoons (½ stick) unsalted butter, melted

1½ cups grated Parmesan cheese, preferably Parmigiano-Reggiano

Thaw the puff pastry for 30 minutes at room temperature. Position the oven racks in the center and top third of the oven. Preheat the oven to 400°F. Have ready 2 rimmed baking sheets, preferably nonstick, otherwise line with parchment paper. Unfold one of the puff pastry sheets and arrange it on a cutting board, with the longer side facing you. Brush both sides generously with melted butter. Sprinkle half of the cheese evenly over one side of the pastry, and then gently press down on the cheese so it adheres to the pastry.

Using a pizza cutter or sharp knife, cut the pastry lengthwise into twelve ½-inch-wide strips. Lifting one strip at a time, transfer to the baking sheet. Starting at one end, twist each strip 8 times to form a spiral breadstick. Press down on both ends of the strip, securing it firmly to the baking sheet. Repeat to form 12 breadsticks. Follow the same method with the second sheet of pastry.

Bake the breadsticks, rotating the pans halfway through the baking time, until crisp and toasty brown, 13 to 15 minutes. Let cool on the pans for 5 minutes. Transfer to a basket or arrange vertically in a tall, wide serving container.

DIPPABLES DO-AHEAD

The breadsticks are best when made the day of serving, but can prepared up to 1 day in advance. Store at room temperature in an airtight container. The breadsticks will lose their crispness if wrapped in plastic wrap or stored in a plastic bag.

Baked Tortilla Chips

Makes about **96 tortilla chips;**
12 to 16 appetizer servings

For cooks who don't like to deep-fry but still want to make homemade chips, baked tortilla chips are a great solution—and they're lower in fat! Crisp and full of flavor, these crunchy triangles warm from the oven will turn any party into a fiesta. Try the baked triangles crusted with poppy and sesame seeds, or make the vibrant chile-lime chips—these are perfect scoopers for any of the chile-fueled salsas and guacamoles in this book.

12 (6- to 8-inch) white or yellow corn tortillas

Vegetable oil for brushing

Kosher salt

Position the oven racks in the center and top third of the oven. Preheat the oven to 400°F.

Using a pastry brush, lightly brush the tortillas on both sides with vegetable oil. Using a sharp knife, cut the tortillas crosswise into 6 or 8 wedges. Arrange the wedges on 2 rimmed baking sheets in a single layer without crowding the pan. (Bake the tortilla chips in batches if they won't all fit.) Bake the tortillas on one side for 5 minutes, and then turn the chips over. Switch the position of the baking sheets and continue baking the chips until they are crisp and just beginning to color, about 5 minutes longer. Sprinkle lightly with salt, transfer to a basket or serving bowl, and serve immediately.

Variations

Seeded Tortilla Chips: In a small bowl, combine ½ cup vegetable oil with 4 teaspoons ground coriander, 2 teaspoons kosher salt, and 1½ tablespoons each of poppy seeds and sesame seeds. Mix well to combine. Generously brush this mixture on one side of each of the tortillas and then cut the tortillas into wedges and bake as directed above.

continued →

Chile-Lime Tortilla Chips: In a small bowl, combine ¼ cup vegetable oil with 2 tablespoons fresh lime juice and ½ teaspoon each of ground coriander, ground cumin, and salt. Add 1 teaspoon each of paprika and chili powder. Mix well to combine. Generously brush this mixture on one side of each of the tortillas and then cut the tortillas into wedges. Bake them on the first side for 7 minutes and then turn over and proceed as directed in the original recipe.

DIPPABLES DO-AHEAD

The tortilla chips are best served within 8 hours of making them. Store uncovered at room temperature and rewarm in the oven just before serving.

Fried Tortilla Chips

Makes about **96 tortilla chips;**
12 to 16 appetizer servings

Store-bought tortilla chips never taste quite the same as the warm and crunchy chips served fresh-from-the-fryer at good Mexican restaurants. Likewise, your guests will indeed notice the difference if you serve these easily prepared homemade chips. When I was experimenting with this recipe, my son invited a group of friends over to try all the different chips I had made. Now they view themselves as chip aficionados, declaring bagged chips as only second best.

12 (6- to 8-inch) white or yellow corn tortillas

About 1½ quarts canola or vegetable oil, for deep-frying

Kosher salt

Using a sharp knife, cut the tortillas crosswise into 6 or 8 wedges. Separate the wedges and let them dry out on the counter while the oil heats. Have ready 2 baking sheets lined with a double thickness of paper towels.

Pour enough oil into a deep, heavy pot, or electric deep-fryer, to come about 3 inches up the sides. (If using an electric deep-fryer, follow the manufacturer's instructions for heating oil.) Heat the oil until the temperature registers 375°F on a deep-frying thermometer.

Frying in small batches, add a handful of tortillas and deep-fry, stirring once or twice, until the chips are light brown and crisp, about 1½ minutes. Using a slotted spoon or wire-mesh skimmer, transfer the chips to the prepared baking sheets to drain. Sprinkle lightly with salt. Continue frying in small batches, checking to make sure the oil is at 375°F before adding another batch.

Transfer to a basket or serving bowl and serve immediately.

DIPPABLES DO-AHEAD

The tortilla chips are best served within 8 hours of making them. Store uncovered at room temperature.

Vegetable Chips

Vegetable chips make terrific party dippers. You can buy a variety of vegetable chips and, of course, potato chips at any supermarket, but as a fun, just-playing-in-the-kitchen activity there is nothing like making hot, crispy-fresh vegetable chips. I've provided you a list of my favorite vegetables to deep-fry—pick and choose—making all of them would feed a crowd. In fact, when I was testing this recipe I did make all of them, looked at the large mound of chips, and decided to heap them into a large, wide basket and serve them to the parents and students sitting on the bleachers at my daughter's varsity basketball game. That was a crowd pleaser!

If you only want to use one or two vegetables, such as potato or sweet potato, to make chips instead of the large assortment I've offered here, then allow a total weight of ¼ to ⅓ pound vegetables per person. Guests never seem to tire of vegetable chips, so be generous in your estimates when shopping; even ½ pound per person won't be too much. They're that good.

3 large red or golden beets

2 large thick carrots

2 russet potatoes

1 or 2 sweet potatoes

1 taro root (see page 15)

1 large yucca (cassava) root (see page 15)

2 large firm zucchini

All-purpose flour, for dusting the zucchini slices

About 1½ quarts canola or vegetable oil, for deep-frying

Kosher salt

Trim the ends of the vegetables and peel them, with the exception of the zucchini, which is left unpeeled. (The potatoes also can be left unpeeled, if desired.) Using a very sharp knife, mandoline, Japanese vegetable slicer, or food processor, slice the vegetables crosswise into paper-thin, $\frac{1}{16}$-inch-thick slices. The carrots and zucchini look best if sliced on the diagonal into very thin, oval slices. Toss the zucchini slices in flour just before frying, shaking off the excess flour. Place the potatoes in a bowl of cold water to keep them from discoloring. When ready to fry the potatoes, drain and blot the potatoes dry with paper towels.

Have ready 2 baking sheets lined with a double thickness of paper towels.

Pour enough oil into a deep, heavy pot, or electric deep-fryer, to come about 3 inches up the sides. (If using an electric deep-fryer, follow the manufacturer's instructions for heating oil.) Heat the oil until the temperature registers 375°F on a deep-frying thermometer.

Fry each vegetable separately and always in small batches. (Fry the beets last, as their juice can discolor the oil.) Add a handful of vegetable slices to the oil and deep-fry, stirring once or twice, until they are golden brown, 2 to 4 minutes. The time will vary slightly for each vegetable. Using a slotted spoon or wire-mesh skimmer, transfer the vegetable chips to the prepared baking sheets to remove excess oil. Sprinkle lightly with salt. Continue frying in small batches, checking to make sure the oil is at 375°F before adding another batch.

Transfer to a basket or serving bowl and serve immediately.

DIPPABLES DO-AHEAD

The vegetable chips are best made just before serving, but can be made up to 6 hours ahead and stored uncovered at room temperature.

Heart-Shaped Apple-Cinnamon Tortilla Chips

Makes about **72 chips;**
12 to 14 dessert servings

For a little whimsy and fun, turn plain flour tortillas into cute and incredibly tasty dessert chips with just a brushing of apple jelly and a sprinkling of cinnamon sugar. Once baked, these chips glisten like jewels and have a pleasing crispness, making them perfect party crunchables for adults or children. Play with different cookie-cutter shapes—hearts are sweet, simple circles look great, and even wide strips work well. These chips are terrific with the Caramel and Dark Rum Fondue (page 89) and the Twistin' in the Tropics Fruit Salsa (page 87).

2 teaspoons ground cinnamon

½ cup sugar

6 (10-inch) flour tortillas

¼ cup apple jelly, melted

Position the oven racks in the center and bottom third of the oven. Preheat the oven to 350°F. Spray the bottom of 2 rimmed baking sheets with vegetable oil cooking spray, or use nonstick baking sheets.

In a small bowl combine the cinnamon and sugar. Using a pastry brush, brush the tortillas generously, on one side only, with the jelly. Using a 2½-inch heart-shaped cookie cutter, round cookie cutter, or any other fun cookie cutter of about the same size, cut the tortillas into shapes. Sprinkle the brushed side generously with sugar and arrange on the baking sheets without crowding. (Bake the tortilla chips in batches if they all won't fit.) Bake until the tortillas are crispy and golden brown, about 12 minutes, switching the position of the baking sheets halfway through the baking time. Transfer to a wire rack to cool. Arrange in a basket or serving bowl and serve immediately.

DIPPABLES DO-AHEAD

The tortilla chips are best served within 8 hours of making them, but can be prepared 1 day in advance and stored in a covered container at room temperature. The chips will soften if stored in plastic bags.

Toasted Pound Cake Crisps

Makes about **46 crisps;**
8 to 10 dessert servings

I never thought about turning pound cake into chips until I was served a strawberry and whipped cream napoleon dessert at a party. Instead of the traditional layers of crisp sweetened puff pastry sheets, they were made of thinly sliced and toasted pound cake. I found myself breaking off pieces of the crisp layers and dipping them in the mounds of whipped cream. A perfect dessert chip! As a delicious alternative to buying a frozen pound cake, you can shop at a bakery for orange or lemon poppy-seed pound cake. Bakery cakes are generally moister than frozen ones, so bake the slices longer for crisp chips. Enjoy these with the Lime Mousse Dip (page 92) and the Bittersweet Chocolate and Grand Marnier Fondue (page 91).

1 loaf (10.75 ounces) frozen all-butter pound cake, thawed, or 1 loaf bakery pound cake

Position the oven racks in the center and top third of the oven. Preheat the oven to 350°F. Have ready 2 rimmed baking sheets.

Using a sharp knife, trim the ends of the pound cake and then cut the cake crosswise into ¼-inch-thick slices. Cut each slice on the diagonal to form 2 triangles. Arrange the slices in a single layer on the baking sheets. Bake until the slices are beginning to turn light brown at the edges, about 5 minutes. Turn the slices over, switch the position of the baking sheets, and bake until the slices just begin to pick up color, about 2 minutes longer. Transfer to a wire rack to cool. Arrange in a basket or serving bowl and serve immediately.

DIPPABLES DO-AHEAD

The pound cake crisps are best served within 8 hours of making them. Store uncovered until serving.

Double-Chocolate Chunk Brownie Chips

Makes **30 brownie chips;**
10 dessert servings

When I was writing my cookbook *Midnight Munchies,* I experimented with mixes to see if I could create brownie "chips" instead of the more typical soft, tender brownies. These are the "chips" and they are divine with both Cherry Garcia Takes a Dip (page 84) and the Chocolate Mocha Mascarpone Dip (page 86). In fact, they're irresistible all by themselves.

Nonstick cooking spray for greasing pan

¼ cup vegetable oil

1 large egg

3 tablespoons water

1 package (15.5 ounces) Pillsbury Chocolate Chunk Thick'n Fudgy Deluxe Brownie mix

Preheat the oven to 350°F. Spray the bottom of a 10-by-15-inch rimmed baking sheet, preferably nonstick, with the cooking spray.

In a bowl, combine the oil, egg, and water and beat with a fork or wooden spoon until well blended. Stir in the brownie mix and beat until well blended. Spread evenly in the prepared pan.

Bake for 20 minutes. Remove from the oven. Use a table knife to score the brownies into about 3-inch squares. Score each square on the diagonal to form 2 triangles. Return to the oven and bake until the brownies are crisp at the edges (but not burnt), about 15 minutes longer. Transfer to a rack and cool in the pan for 10 minutes. Use the edge of a spatula to cut the brownies at the score lines. Lift and remove the brownies from the pan and cool on a rack. They will harden and turn into "chips" as they cool. Arrange on a serving platter or in a basket and serve at room temperature with your choice of dessert dips.

DIPPABLES DO-AHEAD

The brownie chips can be prepared 2 days in advance and stored in a covered container at room temperature. The chips will soften if stored in plastic bags.

Index

Table of Equivalents

The exact equivalents in the following tables have been rounded for convenience.

▪▪▪ Liquid/Dry Measures

U.S.	Metric
¼ teaspoon	1.25 milliliters
½ teaspoon	2.5 milliliters
1 teaspoon	5 milliliters
1 tablespoon (3 teaspoons)	15 milliliters
1 fluid ounce (2 tablespoons)	30 milliliters
¼ cup	60 milliliters
⅓ cup	80 milliliters
½ cup	120 milliliters
1 cup	240 milliliters
1 pint (2 cups)	480 milliliters
1 quart (4 cups, 32 ounces)	960 milliliters
1 gallon (4 quarts)	3.84 liters
1 ounce (by weight)	28 grams
1 pound	454 grams
2.2 pounds	1 kilogram

▪▪▪ Length

U.S.	Metric
⅛ inch	3 millimeters
¼ inch	6 millimeters
½ inch	12 millimeters
1 inch	2.5 centimeters

▪▪▪ Oven Temperature

Fahrenheit	Celsius	Gas
250	120	½
275	140	1
300	150	2
325	160	3
350	180	4
375	190	5
400	200	6
425	220	7
450	230	8
475	240	9
500	260	10